THE ARMOR OF VICTORY

*Exposing the Strategy
of the Evil One*

By Janet M. Magiera

LWM Publications
Light of the Word Ministry

Versions quoted are noted by abbreviations after the verse citation as follows:

AMP: Amplified Bible, The Lockman Foundation, 2015.

AMPC: Amplified Bible (Classic edition), The Lockman Foundation, 1965.

APNT: Aramaic Peshitta New Testament Translation, LWM Publications, 2006.

ESV: English Standard Version, Crossway, a publishing ministry of Good News Publishers, 2001.

GWT: God's Word Translation, God's Word to the Nations Society, 1995

KJV: King James Version of the English Bible, 1769 Blayney edition.

NASB: New American Standard Bible, The Lockman Foundation, 1977.

NET: The NET Bible, Biblical Studies Press, 1996.

NIV: New International Version, Biblica, Inc., 1973.

NLT: New Living Translation, Tyndale House Publishers, 1996.

Copyright © 2017, Janet M. Magiera, 2nd Edition
ISBN 978-0-9820085-6-0

LWM Publications, the publishing house of Light of the Word Ministry
6615 Cool Mountain Drive
Colorado Springs, CO 80923
www.lightofword.org

Acknowledgements

I would like to acknowledge the prayer and financial support of all of the faithful contributors to Light of the Word Ministry, without which I would not have the time to pursue the writing of this or any new publications.

I would also like to specifically thank Janice Booze, Trish Barbera, Ellen Fowler, Sheila Hitchcock and Jan Rawlins for their input spiritually, as well as regarding the grammar and formatting of the book. It was invaluable to me and their encouragement and advice has helped to bring the book to fruition.

And lastly, I would like to thank my fellow ministers in San Diego, Robert and Jeanie Lindfelt, and Barney and Vikki Barnhart, who have continually encouraged me to keep teaching and writing. There are many other ministers around the country who have also been instrumental in helping this book to come to publication. I consider myself to be rich indeed with faithful friends.

I am grateful for the opportunity to teach on this particular subject and thankful to God my Father for his mercy and grace.

Table of Contents

Acknowledgements 5

Table of Contents 7

Introduction ....

    THE ARMOR OF VICTORY 9

Chapter 1..

    THE TRUE TITLE OF OUR ENEMY..................................... 13

Chapter 2 ....

    OUR SPIRITUAL CLOTHING... 20

Chapter 3 ....

    SUIT UP AND STAND 29

Chapter 4 ....

    STRATEGY OF THE EVIL ONE 39

Chapter 5 ....

    OVERVIEW OF THE ARMOR OF VICTORY 44

Chapter 6 ....

    THE BELT OF TRUTH 47

Chapter 7 ....

    THE BREASTPLATE OF JUSTIFICATION 59

Chapter 8..

    THE SANDALS OF THE GOSPEL OF PEACE 69

Chapter 9 ....

    THE SHIELD OF THE NAME OF JESUS CHRIST.................. 79

Chapter 10...

THE HELMET OF REDEMPTION... 91

Chapter 11 ....

THE SWORD OF THE SPIRIT, THE LIVING WORD 101

Chapter 12 ....

THE POWERS THAT BE.. 113

Chapter 13 ....

CASTING DOWN STRONGHOLDS.. 129

Chapter 14 ....

BEING PREPARED IN EVERYTHING, STAND 147

Appendix ....

Other Names of the Evil One 156

Bibliography 157

About the Author.. 163

Introduction
THE ARMOR OF VICTORY

The armor of God is a popular topic, particularly for Sunday School lessons. But why is this concept so vital to the Christian walk? The idea of fighting in a war with armor on is very appealing, as illustrated by the cartoons with Super Heroes like Iron Man and Wonder Woman, but what does it really mean and what is the actual war?

I had been a Christian for a number of years and had seen miracles and healing on numerous occasions. But then in seemingly similar situations, I did not witness the same victorious results. Questioning and pondering the reasons for this led me to extensively study the armor of God and to learn about spiritual warfare. I have found the field to be rich with positive teaching, but also that many people had the same questions as I did about engaging in this warfare. It was never my intention to write another book on the topic of spiritual warfare when there were already so many good resources, contributed by very knowledgeable workmen of God's Word. Yet these unanswered questions regarding how to walk in victory led me to dig into God's Word for understanding and direction. This book is the result of much of that research.

As God graciously unfolded some key understanding in my heart, I began to see that there was a need for every Christian who wanted to walk in victory to master this topic and to learn how the armor is applied in the Christian life.

There are two main areas that this study will clarify:

1. The action believers are responsible for and what is provided in our power base in Christ.
2. The nature of the spiritual warfare and the Enemy's strategy.

God always causes us to triumph in Christ. Old things are passed away and all things have become new. We are filled with the love of God and the Spirit of Christ. Since this is true, why should we learn about the armor of God?

The answer to this question will unfold as we carefully study the scriptures that are set forth in Ephesians 6, the passage that describes in detail the armor of God. This passage is not an isolated illustration of a soldier, but a summary of all of who we are in Christ and must be understood in light of the conduct (walk) to which God calls every believer.

God's plan of salvation is fulfilled in Christ and now everyone who believes on Christ has received an overwhelming victory in him.

Romans 8:37 NASB
But in all these things we overwhelmingly conquer through Him who loved us.

This victory is won, but it needs to be appropriated into our lives on a day by day basis. In order to appropriate the victory, we need to put on the whole armor of God. This is necessary for every believer to do, so it is critical for us to understand more about HOW we are to fight in the battle.

We ARE at war and the warfare is spiritual!

Ephesians 6:10 KJV .
Finally, my brethren, be strong in the Lord and in the power of his might.

"The power of his might" is a synopsis of all that God has made available to us in our Lord Jesus Christ. To put on the whole armor of God is to be clothed with HIS power in practical application. Understanding the armor enables us to determine what we need to do with what we have been given to be victorious in the struggle against the principalities and powers on high.

God has vast resources of might that we can put into operation in our lives. But his might does not work in me as I sit passively. His might works in me only as I rely on it and step out to do my part. Which is my part and which is HIS? Now is the time to learn what God says we should do and what he has already done in Christ.

I invite you to prayerfully consider the following pages to learn how to practically apply the armor of God to win victories not only for yourself, but for your family and fellow believers in the body of Christ.

Chapter 1
THE TRUE TITLE OF OUR ENEMY

1 Peter 5:8 ESV
Be sober-minded; be watchful. Your adversary the devil prowls around like a roaring lion, seeking someone to devour.

Unfortunately, because many people are ignorant of the Devil's nature and schemes, they are easily devoured. The New Living Translation of the beginning of this verse says, "Stay alert! Watch out for your great enemy." In order to watch, we must first wake up! That does not mean that we give glory or honor to the Devil, but we do need to expose his methods and learn how to be armed against his prowling attacks.

Why should you study or read a book that examines the Adversary's plans and schemes? Isn't he some gruesome being with horns, a tail, and (of course) a pitchfork which he uses to pitch people into his jail called hell? Why should we learn about that? Shouldn't we concentrate on who we are in Christ and forget about the Enemy? The Bible is full of references to Satan and his demons and God exhorts us not to be "ignorant of his devices" (2 Corinthians 2:11b).

This study will not only present the strategy, devices and tactics of the Enemy's army, but also show definitively that the armor of God in Christ Jesus is the most complete and effective way to combat all of the Enemy's attacks. So far, I have used three names that are given to the Devil: Satan, the Adversary, and the Enemy. We will probe these names more closely and see how they actually exemplify his evil character and sinister purposes.

This area of the names of the Enemy is the first area where we should not be ignorant. Most well-meaning Christians interchange-ably use the names Satan, the Devil, and the Adversary, but these are specific names, each of which shows only one of his major devices. When we understand his specific names, his tactics will be exposed.

The name that summarizes his whole strategy is the "Evil One." I came to this conclusion by endeavoring to study the individual names like Satan and Devil. The term "evil" or "wicked" emerged as a broad umbrella under which other names were also associated, such as "prince of the power of the air" and "devourer." These additional names were descriptive of his activities and showed his characteristics. The one most often used was "Evil One" to convey all the different types of activities. Please note the Appendix on page 156 for a list of the additional names and titles of the Evil One.

You are beginning to see that I am capitalizing the names of the Evil One. In the *Aramaic Peshitta New Testament Translation*, this name is written as Evil [one] because the word is being used as a noun and the "one" needs to be supplied in English. I have capitalized the names we will be discussing in this book because I want them to be noticed as proper nouns, which in English are always capitalized. In no way am I glorifying or honoring our Enemy by doing this.

The Evil One in Greek is a specific phrase, **ho poneros**. It is an adjective for evil used with a definite article, which changes the adjective to a noun, referring to the "active worker out of evil."[1] Bullinger distinguished this phrase in his concordance and its uses line up with the Aramaic translation.

An example is in the Lord's Prayer. The King James Version translates the Greek phrase **ho poneros** as "evil." It should be the Evil One. Many modern translations have the "evil one."

Matthew 6:13 KJV
And lead us not into temptation, but deliver us from evil: For thine is the kingdom, and the power, and the glory, for ever. Amen.

Matthew 6:13 NET
And do not lead us into temptation, but deliver us from the evil one.

---

[1] Bullinger, *A Critical Lexicon and Concordance*, p. 262.

The Lord Jesus Christ is the one who broadly exposed the Evil One for who he was – the author of all sickness and oppression. He is dedicated to evil of every kind.

Acts 10:38 APNT
Concerning Jesus, who was from Nazareth, whom God anointed with the Holy Spirit and with power. And this is he who traveled around and healed those who were oppressed by the Evil [one], because God was with him.

"To oppress" could be translated from the Greek as "to exercise harsh control over, to use one's power against one." That is certainly the goal of the Evil One: to have control over people. But the Aramaic word for "oppressed" in Acts 10 and its companion Hebrew word in the Old Testament paint an even broader picture. The Aramaic is **neka**, and the definitions range from "harm, wound, injure, and hurt" to "crush, beat, kill, slay and destroy." The word picture is "to crush seeds in one's hand (as for making spices) or with a mortar and pestle." The point is to totally crush the seeds. [2]

Isaiah describes what the "wicked" or "wicked one" had done and whose authority will be broken in the future. He used a club or staff to strike people with unceasing blows.

Isaiah 14:5-6 ESV
*The LORD has broken the staff of the wicked, the scepter of rulers, that struck [**nakah**] the peoples in wrath with unceasing blows, that ruled the nations in anger with unrelenting persecution.*

There are at least 14 passages which identify the Evil One. Here are just a few. The verse from John is from Jesus' prayer right before his death.

2 Thessalonians 3:3 APNT
But the LORD is faithful, who will keep you and rescue you from the Evil [one].

---

[2] Jeff Benner, *Ancient Hebrew Lexicon of the Bible*, p. 184.

1 John 2:13-14 APNT
I am writing to you, fathers, because you have known him who is from the beginning. I am writing to you, young men, because you have overcome the Evil [one]. I have written to you, young boys, because you have known the Father.
I have written to you, fathers, because you have known him who was from the beginning. I have written to you, young men, because you are strong and the word of God lives in you and you have overcome the Evil [one].

John 17:15 APNT
I do not pray that you should take them from the world, but that you would keep them from the Evil [one],

As we go through this study, you will become more aware of the personal nature of the Evil One and understand that although he does have some power, the power of Jesus our Messiah is far greater.

The Evil One is not an impersonal influence, but rather a real spiritual being created by God as the angel of light, who is now a fallen angel. Because he is a being with supernatural powers created by the one true God, he has limitations. All angels are spirit beings with spiritual capabilities given to them by God and they are not omnipotent or omnipresent. They have a limited scope of knowledge and presence, unlike God who knows all things and is everywhere present.

Psalm 148:2, 5 KJV
Praise ye him, all his angels: praise ye him, all his hosts.
Let them praise the name of the LORD: for he commanded, and they were created.

THE NAME "LUCIFER"

The Evil One was an anointed cherub. The descriptions given of him before his fall shows that he was originally full of wisdom and perfect in beauty. He was chosen to be one of the cherubim who guarded the throne of God. God instructed Moses to have a representation of the cherubim made to cover the ark of the covenant to guard the mercy seat with outstretched wings and faces toward it (Exodus 25:20). Since the ark of the covenant represented the presence of God, the cherubim are angelic beings that are in the closest proximity to God.

Ezekiel 28 describes that Lucifer walked on the holy mountain of God.

Ezekiel 28:14-15 KJV
Thou art the anointed cherub that covereth; and I have set thee so: thou wast upon the holy mountain of God; thou hast walked up and down in the midst of the stones of fire.
Thou wast perfect in thy ways from the day that thou wast created, till iniquity was found in thee.

The word in Hebrew for "iniquity" is **evel.** *The Theological Wordbook of the Old Testament* says that "the basic meaning of this root means to deviate from a right standard, to act contrary to what is right." Ezekiel 28 goes on to describe what happened to this beautiful cherub.

Ezekiel 28:16-17 ESV
In the abundance of your trade you were filled with violence in your midst, and you sinned; so I cast you as a profane thing from the mountain of God, and I destroyed you, O guardian cherub, from the midst of the stones of fire.
Your heart was proud because of your beauty; you corrupted your wisdom for the sake of your splendor. I cast you to the ground; I exposed you before kings, to feast their eyes on you.

The Evil One was a cherub whose demise was due to his willful pride. His haughty desire was to be like the Most High who is worthy of all praise and worship, rather than to offer praise and worship along with the other cherubim and angels. His pride drove him to seek not only a position above all of the angels, but a throne that would be loftier than the Most High God.

Isaiah 14:12-14 NASB
How you have fallen from heaven, O star of the morning, son of the
dawn! You have been cut down to the earth, You who have weakened
the nations!
But you said in your heart, 'I will ascend to heaven; I will raise my
throne above the stars of God, And I will sit on the mount of assembly
in the recesses of the north.'
'I will ascend above the heights of the clouds; I will make myself like
the Most High.'

The phrase "star of the morning" in the King James Version is "Lucifer" which is a Latin term meaning, literally, "light-bringer." This is an incorrect title for the Evil One. This name, Lucifer, came as a translation of the Hebrew, **heylel,** which means "shining one." The verb **halal** is interesting because it is a homonym, a verb with two meanings. It means "to shine," but also "to boast or praise." The noun can be positive praise and celebration or negative boasting. I believe that the point of calling him **heylel** is that he was a praiser who turned into a boaster. He wanted privileges and recognition far more distinguishing for himself than God had already generously provided. He wanted to be more than he was created to be. This is actually a summation of his character: boastful pride.

There is no word for "star" in Hebrew. The second phrase, "son of the dawn," may actually be a title or another description of who this "shining one" was before his fall. "Son of the dawn" is a Hebrew expression which refers to the planet Venus, which is also called "the morning star." Venus rises brightly in the morning, but then falls rapidly out of sight. This entire passage in Isaiah is literally referring to the King of Babylon, Nebuchadnezzar, a quite powerful king who was highly exalted in the eyes of men, yet plummeted to the depths of depravity in a very short period of time (Daniel 4:30-33).

Isaiah 14:4 KJV
That thou shalt take up this proverb against the king of Babylon, and
say, How hath the oppressor ceased! the golden city ceased!

Isaiah's dual reference to a literal king and to the Evil One is confirmed in the book of Revelation when this boasting angel (Lucifer) will have his actual physical demise and the city of Babylon will be destroyed.

Revelation 18:10 KJV
Standing afar off for the fear of her torment, saying, Alas, alas, that great city Babylon, that mighty city! for in one hour is thy judgment come.

So far we have seen that the true title of our Enemy is the Evil One. There is nothing good about him. His purposes are always to crush and eventually destroy. He is filled with willful pride and uses any means possible to turn people away from God, as he himself did when he rebelled against God. His overall purpose is always to bring worship and honor to himself, rather than to God.

Chapter 2
OUR SPIRITUAL CLOTHING

There are many who have not yet realized this truth – but we are engaged in a spiritual battle! Against what or whom? The army of the Evil One! If you are already aware of the ongoing battle, you probably know that it is not always easy to continually emerge a victor in the daily skirmishes and relentless attacks of everyday life. How do we achieve and maintain victory in this persistent battle? We realize victory when we dress ourselves according to God's direction with "our spiritual clothing."

In the last chapter, the emphasis was on the identity of the Evil One and his basic purpose. We are now going to take a look at the overall principle of how to be "more than conquerors" over him.

Romans 8:36-37 APNT
As it is written: because of you every day we are dying and we are counted as lambs to slaughter.
On the contrary, in all these [things] we are victorious by way of him who loved us.

The Amplified Version of verse 37 is "Yet in all these things we are more than conquerors *and* gain an overwhelming victory..." We <u>have</u> the victory!!! "Through him who loved us" refers to God by way of what he provided for us in Christ. God loved us so much that he gave us the greatest gift possible, the full measure of the gift of Christ, which is the indwelling gift of the Spirit, "Christ in you" within every believer (Colossians 1:27). This gift of Christ is energized via nine manifestations (1 Corinthians 12:7-11). This amazing gift is the basis for our victory.

Ephesians 4:7 APNT
Now to each one of us is given grace according to the measure of the gift of Christ.

In Luke 24:49, Jesus told his disciples to wait in Jerusalem until they were "clothed with power from on high." Then, as Acts 2 describes, on the day of Pentecost they were filled with the Spirit (they received spiritual power) and began to speak with other tongues. When we are born again, we also receive the gift of Christ and are clothed with HIS power.

The gift from God is described in different ways and we need to understand this gift in order to relate to the imagery used about the armor of God. God, who is Spirit, gave of who he is, holiness and spirit. That is why the gift is literally "the spirit of holiness" in Aramaic. The word "holy" is not an adjective, but a noun describing what the gift is.

Acts 2:38 APNT
Simon said to them, "Repent and be baptized, each one of you, in the name of the Lord Jesus for the forgiveness of sins, so that you will receive the gift of the Holy Spirit [spirit of holiness]. *"*

The spiritual clothing that we receive as a gift when we are born again is an endowment of power. In the prayer in Ephesians 1, Paul prays for the believers to know this power.

Ephesians 1:17-21 NET
I pray that the God of our Lord Jesus Christ, the Father of glory, may give you spiritual wisdom and revelation in your growing knowledge of him,
since the eyes of your heart have been enlightened – so that you may know what is the hope of his calling, what is the wealth of his glorious inheritance in the saints,
and what is the incomparable greatness of his power toward us who believe, as displayed in the exercise of his immense strength.
This power he exercised in Christ when he raised him from the dead and seated him at his right hand in the heavenly realms
far above every rule and authority and power and dominion and every name that is named, not only in this age but also in the one to come.

There are other ways the gift is described in the epistles. It is being "baptized into Christ" (Galatians 3:27), "the inward man" (Romans 7: 22), "the new man" (Ephesians 4:24, Colossians 3:10), "Christ in you" (Colossians 1:27), and the "measure of the gift of Christ" (Ephesians 4:7).

Ephesians 2 describes where the gift comes from. There are no works that man can perform in order to receive the gift. It is the gift from God deposited within every believer at the time of the new birth, and it is "not of yourselves."

Ephesians 2:8-10 KJV:
For by grace are ye saved through faith; and that not of yourselves: it is the gift of God:
Not of works, lest any man should boast,
For we are his workmanship, created in Christ Jesus unto good works, which God hath before ordained that we should walk in them.

What are we to do with this gift? We need to "put it on." The Greek word is **enduo** and the Aramaic word is **lebesh**. Both words can be literal, "to put on clothes." There are also eight places where the usage of "to put on" is talking about putting on the new spiritual body we will have when Christ returns. Luke 24:49 and Galatians 3:27, two verses mentioned above, refer to what we have been given in Christ. The other uses have to do with what to put on in our minds. We have received spiritual clothing to use. Now we must clothe ourselves with it in our minds. The clothing is given to us spiritually, but it is not utilized until it is put on in our minds.

We can understand more about what it means to "put on" by seeing what to "put off" means. "Put off" means to "strip off, strip away, plunder," or "carry off as booty." Ephesians 4:22 says "that ye put off concerning the former conversation the old man, which is corrupt according to the deceitful lusts." The old man is a concept to portray old ways of life. Since "put on" has to do with putting on things in our minds, "put off" has to do with taking off old or worn-out clothes in our minds.

22

Imagine that you have just completed a five-mile run, the last four of which were in a cold, driving rain on a slippery, muddy road. Once you finally arrive home, how long will it take you to shed your dirt-drenched running clothes? When the verb "put on" is used, however, it depicts a different picture – that of careful dressing, as though you were going to the most momentous party of the year. Everything you choose to wear is coordinated and you have it all laid out, having given much thought, effort and time in preparation. That is to "put on" – carefully clothe yourself piece by piece and pay attention to all of the details.

So what are we to clothe ourselves with in our minds? We need to look at three key phrases.

Put on the Lord Jesus Christ

Romans 13:14 KJV
But put ye on the Lord Jesus Christ, and make not provision for the flesh, to fulfil the lusts thereof.

Put on the New Man

Ephesians 4:24 KJV
And that ye put on the new man, which after God is created in righteousness and true holiness.

Colossians 3:10 KJV
And have put on the new man, which is renewed in knowledge after the image of him that created him:

Put on the Armor

Romans 13:12 KJV
The night is far spent, the day is at hand: let us therefore cast off the works of darkness, and let us put on the armour of light.

Ephesians 6:11 KJV
Put on the whole armour of God, that ye may be able to stand against
the wiles of the devil.

Ephesians 6:13 KJV
Wherefore take unto you the whole armour of God, that ye may be
able to withstand in the evil day, and having done all, to stand.

Romans 13:12-14 is the key to understanding how putting on "the armor of light" is the same as putting on "the Lord Jesus Christ." In math, if a = b and c = b, then a = c. 1 John 1:5 states that God is light, so "the armor of light" is the same as "the armor of God." The new man is "Christ in you," so to put on the Lord Jesus Christ is to put on the new man. All three phrases – put on the Lord Jesus Christ, put on the new man and put on the armor of God – are equal to each other. They are different images used to depict the same truth, so that we can understand from several perspectives what we are to put on.

The whole armor is the complete gift-wrapped package of all of the power of Christ, which is the full measure of the stature of Christ. Since the power of Christ is the major topic of the epistles, the section in Ephesians 6:10-18 is not an isolated illustration, but a summary of all that we have been given. Bible commentator, Charles Ellicott, puts it succinctly:

> ...if "to put on the armour of light" is to "put on the Lord Jesus Christ," it follows that the various parts of the defensive armour are the various parts of the image of the Lord Jesus Christ; hence they are properly His, and are through His gift appropriated by us. [3]

Paul wrote the epistle of Ephesians in prison in Rome, where he was probably bound by a chain to a Roman soldier throughout the day. If he was under house arrest, soldiers were guarding him at all times.

---

[3] Charles Ellicott, *Layman's Handy Bible Commentary on the Bible*, p. 228.

He had plenty of time to study their armor and God showed him the spiritual analogy.

"Armor" is translated from the Greek word **panoplia** and the Aramaic word **zaina**. "Panoply," our English word transcribed straight from the Greek, means "a full suit of armor" or "something forming a protective covering." **Zaina** is used not only of military weaponry and armor, but also more generically as equipment or instruments. The most important point is not that it is armor, but rather that each piece is crucial to being fully prepared. A soldier would not consider leaving any part of his "panoply" at home or in his tent. He also needed to know what to do with each piece of his equipment. The Aramaic translation makes this particularly clear.

Ephesians 6:13 APNT
Because of this, put on the whole armor of God, so that you will be able to engage the Evil [one] and, being prepared in everything, you will stand firm.

The passage in Ephesians 6 regarding putting on the armor of God is the key study of this book. By understanding this section clearly, we will be in the best position to become the "more than conquerors" referred to in Romans 8:37. We need to experience putting on the armor of God, which is to put on the Lord Jesus Christ and his power. Then we will be able to stand boldly facing the Evil One without fear.

STRENGTHENED IN THE LORD

We rely on the power of the Spirit, Christ in us, not our own strength. Many people quote a portion of the scripture from Philippians 4:13 that says "I can do all things." Then the reality of our own failed strength hits. The Aramaic translation of this verse is simple to understand and summarizes the mindset of the believer who has put on his spiritual clothing.

Philippians 4:13 APNT
I find strength for everything in Christ who strengthens me.

We need to find the strength, not in ourselves but rather, in CHRIST. The first verse regarding the armor describes this strengthening as being strengthened in the Lord.

Ephesians 6:10 APNT
From now on, my brothers, be strong in our Lord and in the immensity of his power.

Whose power? The power of all that Christ is in us. Colossians 2:10 says that we are complete in Christ.

The phrase "from now on" or "finally" reminds us that we cannot take this section of Ephesians out of context. We must consider all that has been stated prior to this verse which describes who we are in Christ and the life God calls every believer to live. The Greek for "from now on" could be translated "in summary." This passage about the armor of God is a summary of what God revealed in the epistles about our standing in Christ.

"Be strong" means to be strengthened. This verb is passive in both Greek and Aramaic, which means that the emphasis is not on our own ability to be strong, but on the Lord's. The strengthening happens to us as we rely on it. We can understand this physically. A man who has a certain reserve of strength (power) exercises his physical body so that he can have stronger muscles. As he exercises, he actually stresses his existing muscles. The old muscle tissue is torn down and new, stronger tissue develops in its place. God's power works similarly in us as we actually use it; we build spiritual strength by putting the spiritual power within us into operation.

The word "immensity" has to do with authority. Its comparable Hebrew root is used in the book of Esther when Mordecai was given authority to act in the name of King Ahasuerus. He used this authoritative power in everything he did for King Ahasuerus. We can compare this kind of authority to the CEO of a large corporation (our smaller-scale example of a king). When he declares a ruling or institutes a policy, his word is final and everyone in the corporation is obliged to carry out his policy.

We are to be strengthened in our Lord and in his authoritative power. Jesus was made Lord in the resurrection and this kind of power is also resurrection power. It is the same power that raised Jesus Christ from the dead.

Romans 1:3-4 NASB
Concerning His Son, who was born of a descendant of David according to the flesh,
who was declared the Son of God with power by the resurrection from the dead, according to the Spirit of holiness, Jesus Christ our Lord.

Now we are sons of God with power! At one time I had a vision showing me what this kind of power was like. Before me was a huge steel door from the ceiling to the floor; the door was massive – at least eight feet thick. Then there appeared a gigantic bit, like the long spiral type used in a high-powered drill. The bit was all set up to go through the huge, thick wall. The only thing required of me was to turn the drill on to activate the bit. It easily penetrated the wall, not because of my strength but because of the strength of the drill. It didn't matter that the wall was thick. It didn't matter that it was made out of steel. What mattered was that the power of the drill was greater than the size and strength of the steel wall it was going through. That's the kind of power we are talking about here – the immensity of his power. It operates, it moves, it goes through seemingly impervious objects and as a result, something amazing happens! The power is not static, but dynamic and forceful.

We often encounter two fallacies when considering the nature of this immense power of the Lord: a) that we do not need to do anything in order for the power to be energized and b) that we can do mighty works in our own strength without relying on HIS power. Neither viewpoint is correct. The truth is that we need to exercise and rely on his authoritative power and THEN we will be able to stand against the attacks of the Evil One.

Let's reread verse 10. "Be strong in our Lord and in the immensity of his power." Another way you could translate "immensity" is "overpower." The armor is not our might or power. The dynamic power referred to is the power that has been given to us in Christ. God's power works in me as I step out to exercise it and put it into operation. Our spiritual clothing is complete, powerful, immense and strong! Our job is to clothe ourselves with this power by putting on the full armor provided for us in our Lord Jesus Christ.

Chapter 3
SUIT UP AND STAND

In the last chapter, we learned that the spiritual clothing we have is the power of Christ in us. This is the armor that we must put on. Now what are we to do once clothed?

Before proceeding to study the actual pieces of the armor, two points are extremely important to understand.

1. Putting on the armor of God enables us to stand against the tactics of the Devil.
2. Our struggle is not against people (flesh and blood) but rather against spiritual foes.

Ephesians 6:11 APNT
And put on the whole armor of God, so that you may be able to stand against the tactics of the Accuser.

The word translated "tactics" in Aramaic is **tsenetha** and is only used here. Many times when we look at the root verb, we will understand the noun better. The verb is **tsana** and means "to contrive, plot; to act cunningly, skillfully, artfully."[4]

Ephesians 4:14 APNT
*And we should not be babies, who are shaken and blown about by every wind of the deceitful teachings of men, who in their craftiness are plotting [**tsana**] to deceive.*

The Evil One has specific tactics which are designed to deceive people. These "schemes" (as the Greek word is translated in the English Standard Version of verse 11) are what he has used since the beginning with Adam and Eve. For many thousands of years, he has employed these schemes to entrap mankind. We need to know what

---

[4] Payne Smith, *A Compendious Syriac Dictionary,* p. 481.

these tactics are and how to combat them. The specific descriptions of these tactics will be discussed when we study the individual pieces of the armor.

STAND AGAINST

The word "stand" is a rich concept to study. The Aramaic word means simply "to rise up" and after rising up, "hold your place." A person who is standing is firm and fixed in that position. In both Greek and Aramaic, the word "stand" is used three times in succession in Ephesians 6:11-14; we saw the first use above in verse 11. This figure of speech of repetition emphasizes the importance of standing and of putting on the armor in order to be able to stand with boldness and confidence.

Ephesians 6:11, 13-14a APNT
And put on the whole armor of God, so that you may be able to stand against the tactics of the Accuser.
Because of this, put on the whole armor of God, so that you will be able to engage the Evil [one] and, being prepared in everything, you will stand firm.
Therefore, stand....

We have been equipped with the power of the Lord Jesus Christ so that we may withstand the Evil One (and in the evil day as in the King James Version). We need to clothe ourselves – suit up – and then being prepared or equipped with everything we need, continue to stand. The Church epistles include many other exhortations to stand. Here are just a few:

1 Corinthians 16:13 ESV
Be watchful, stand firm in the faith, act like men, be strong.

Galatians 5:1 ESV
For freedom Christ has set us free; stand firm therefore, and do not submit again to a yoke of slavery.

Philippians 4:1 ESV
Therefore, my brothers, whom I love and long for, my joy and crown,
stand firm thus in the Lord, my beloved.

2 Thessalonians 2:15 ESV
So then, brothers, stand firm and hold to the traditions that you were
taught by us, either by our spoken word or by our letter.

Watchman Nee in his book *Sit, Walk, Stand,* sums up our stand in this way:

> Satan's primary object is not to get us to sin, but simply to make it easy for us to do so by getting us off the ground of perfect triumph onto which the Lord has brought us. Through the avenue of the head or of the heart, through our intellect or our feelings, he assaults our rest in Christ or our walk in the Spirit. But for every point of his attack, defensive armor is provided – the helmet and the breastplate, the girdle and the shoes – while over all is the shield of faith to turn aside his fiery darts....Because victory is His [Christ's], therefore it is ours. If only we will not try to gain the victory, but simply to maintain it, then we shall see the Enemy utterly routed.[5]

"Stand" in Ephesians 6 has the sense of "drawing up a military formation for combat." In verse 13 it refers to the triumphant stance of the victor.[6] The military formation we stand in together with our fellow soldiers in the body of Christ is as already victorious, not trying to gain a victory.

Many Christians envision a distorted concept of spiritual warfare. They picture themselves as soldiers in an army assaulting the kingdom of hell or perhaps on patrol, expecting to discover demons and spiritual enemies lurking in the underbrush of life's forests. These

---

[5] Watchman Nee, *Sit, Walk, Stand,* pp. 44-45.
[6] Walter Wink, *Naming the Powers,* p. 87.

are hardly accurate depictions of the spiritual battlefield. Our battlefield is in our minds and our purpose for putting on the armor is to be able to stand opposite the Evil One in our already-won victory. We stand against the devices and tactics of the Evil One in our minds by refusing to entertain any thoughts of defeat.

Let's look at something intriguing the Lord said in Matthew 16.

Matthew 16:18 ESV
And I tell you, you are Peter, and on this rock I will build my church, and the gates of hell shall not prevail against it.

What is Jesus talking about in this verse? Investigating Biblical customs will shed some light on the phrase "gates of hell." In the ancient world, the city council and judges gathered together at the gates of the city; this is where the city life was planned and organized. In using this phrase, Jesus spoke of the ultimate strategy of the Enemy to defeat every man – and that strategy was death. No man had ever been able to escape the place of death, also called Sheol (translated "hell" in the King James Version). By his death and resurrection, Jesus delivered us from what the Evil One had used to hold men in bondage for their whole lives.

Hebrews 2:14-15 KJV
Forasmuch then as the children are partakers of flesh and blood, he also himself likewise took part of the same; that through death he might destroy him that had the power of death, that is, the devil;
And deliver them who through fear of death were all their lifetime subject to bondage.

From the fall of man onward, the Enemy set his army in array to lure men into his traps and ultimately death. Jesus offered his sinless life as a substitute payment for Adam's sin. When Jesus Christ submitted to the death of the cross, he was buried – but he did not stay in the grave. God raised him up from the dead and thereby obliterated the power of the Devil. God's power over death and the grave was greater than the Enemy's greatest weapon.

After Jesus Christ was raised from the dead, he disarmed the principalities and powers and brought the Evil One to open shame.

Colossians 2:13-15 ESV
And you, who were dead in your trespasses and the uncircumcision of your flesh, God made alive together with him, having forgiven us all our trespasses,
by canceling the record of debt that stood against us with its legal demands. This he set aside, nailing it to the cross.
He disarmed the rulers and authorities and put them to open shame, by triumphing over them in him.

The Amplified Version of verse 15 states, "When He had disarmed the rulers and authorities [those supernatural forces of evil operating against us], He made a public example of them [exhibiting them as captives in His triumphal procession], having triumphed over them through the cross." This is an important truth that we need to embed deep in our hearts: we stand in a place of victory and the rulers and authorities are already disarmed!

THE STRUGGLE

Ephesians 6:12 ESV
For we do not wrestle against flesh and blood, but against the rulers, against the authorities, against the cosmic powers over this present darkness, against the spiritual forces of evil in the heavenly places.

We do not wrestle against people. The phrase "flesh and blood" stands for men: that includes, for example, a cranky boss, an overzealous policeman, a rebellious child, etc. All people, we included, may be used by the Evil One to promote his tactics, but our fight is never against people.

The term "wrestle" in verse 12 seems incongruous to introduce into a passage that is using a soldier analogy. Wrestling happened in the Roman arenas and certainly no wrestler would be wearing a full suit of armor for this sport. The Greek word **pale** is used only once, in this passage. Though it means "wrestling," this word can also be defined as "struggling."[7] The word **pale** in Greek is used to describe the hand-to-hand combat of soldiers, combat that requires both struggling and striving. Thayer has an interesting definition: *"wrestling* is a contest between two in which each endeavors to throw the other, and which is decided when the victor is able to.... hold him (the opponent) down with his hand upon his neck."[8]

The Aramaic verb for "to wrestle" is **katash**. Some of the various definitions are "to strive, fight, compete, contend, dispute, and endeavor." The noun based on this verb is used in Ephesians 6:12 and thus is translated, "your struggle is not with flesh and blood."

Who are we struggling against?

Ephesians 6:12 APNT
Because your struggle is not with flesh and blood, but with rulers and with authorities and with the possessors of this dark world and with the evil spirits that are under heaven.

There are four groups described in this verse that we struggle against. These are:

1. Principalities (rulers)
2. Powers (authorities)
3. Rulers of darkness (possessors of this dark world)
4. Wicked spirits (evil spirits)

When I was originally studying the armor of God, I compared it to our modern military armed forces. However, because the modern military is very complicated with various branches – the Marine Corps, the Air Force, the Navy and the Army – the analogy did not

---

[7] Bullinger, *A Critical Lexicon and Concordance,* p. 906.
[8] *The New Thayer's Greek English Lexicon,* p. 474.

hold up. I eventually found that the Roman army had a very simple structure, which parallels the army of the Evil One.

COMPARISON WITH THE ROMAN ARMY

The Roman legions had four main levels of ranks: legates, tribunes, centurions and legionaries. There were some variations of the titles throughout the history of the Roman Empire, but these were the main ranks. A legion was under the command of a legate who acted as the equivalent of a general in modern military terms. Under each legate there were six tribunes who commanded the cohorts. A tribune was an officer of the Roman army who ranked below the legate and above the centurion. The tribunes were also called chiliarchs, because originally they would have commanded 1000 men.[9] Claudius Lysias, who rescued Paul from the crowd in Jerusalem was of the "band" stationed at the fortress near the temple; he was a tribune over the cohort stationed there (Acts 21:31).

Roman Army	Modern Military	Army of the Evil One
Legate	General	Principality
Tribune	Captain	Power
Centurion	Sergeant	Ruler
Legionary	Private	Wicked spirit

A cohort was composed of six centuries which consisted of 80-100 men each. The centurions were the officers who commanded men on a day-to-day basis, both in war and in camp. A number of centurions are mentioned in the New Testament, most notably Cornelius in Caesarea. He belonged to a cohort called the Italian band (Acts 10:1). Originally the Italian band had been formed in Rome of freed slaves who received citizenship.[10]

The remaining soldiers were called legionaries. They were the regular soldiers in the lowest rank.

---

[9] www.warhistoryonline.com/ancient-history
[10] *Holman Illustrated Bible Dictionary*, p. 314.

35

The four main ranks of the Roman legion compare to the ranks of the Evil One's army. The numbers of men in each section of the Roman army are not important in the comparison, but the levels of the ranks of the legion are the same as the ranks of the Evil One's army.

PRINCIPALITIES

There are six main principalities. These principalities are the names the Evil One hides behind. He is the commander-in-chief, but he has six legates or generals. A principality simply means ruler, or "the person or thing that commences, the first person or thing in a series, the leader." [11] The Greek word is **arche**. When **arche** refers to a ruler or magistrate of a spiritual nature, it is called a principality. These rulers hold the highest and loftiest rank. They are the leaders. The principalities are Beelzebub, the Devil (also called the Accuser), the Dragon, Satan, Belial and the Serpent. These will be discussed in detail in the following chapters on the pieces of armor.

POWERS

Powers are like the tribunes; they are responsible for leading the implementation of the Enemy's war strategy. The word "power" in Greek is **exousia** and carries a connotation that refers to both supernatural and natural government. [12] There are two aspects of this power: 1) the ability to act or produce an effect and 2) the possession of authority over others. [13] This is a good summary of the word "power," whether the context is natural or supernatural. Jesus had this kind of power.

Matthew 7:29 KJV
For he taught them as one having authority [**exousia**], *and not as the scribes.*

---

[11] *The New Thayer's Greek English Lexicon*, p. 77.
[12] Cindy Jacobs, *Possessing the Gates of the Enemy*, p. 228.
[13] *Holman Illustrated Bible Dictionary*, p. 1318.

Exousia is also used to describe devil spirits when used in the plural. There are only 13 specific spirits that have been named in the Bible. They are defined by "spirit of..." In the chapter on *The Powers That Be* we will look at these names in detail.

RULERS OF THE DARKNESS

These rulers are like the centurions. They control the day-to-day operation of the army and are in charge of the legionaries. In Ephesians, these are called in Greek **kosmokrator,** which means "world ruler." **Kosmokrator** was technically used in Greek to describe certain aspects of the military. The word depicts "raw power that has been harnessed and put into some kind of order."[14] The Aramaic word for "rulers" here means "possessors." Certain demonic forces amass in different regions of the world, to fortify particular kinds of evil. They control groups of devil spirits who are all focused on similar outcomes.

For example, the ancient city of Pergamos was described in Revelation 2:13 as "where Satan's throne is." In *Unger's Bible Dictionary* it describes Pergamos as "greatly addicted to idolatry and its grove, which was one of the wonders of the place, was filled with statues and altars....devoted to sensual worship."[15] There were world rulers who dominated that city and there was a concentrated mass of demons dedicated to promoting that kind of evil.

The sphere of action is "this darkness," i.e. the morally corrupt state of our present existence."[16] As the centurions of the Roman army, their job is to accomplish the will of their superiors.

---

[14] Rick Renner, *Spiritual Weapons to Defeat the Enemy*, p. 40.
[15] *Unger's Bible Dictionary*, p. 844.
[16] *International Standard Bible Encyclopedia*, 7443 "ruler."

WICKED SPIRITS

The last category of the Evil One's army is called "wicked spirits from on high." They are called evil spirits, unclean spirits, devil spirits, or demons. I believe that they are the equivalent to the legionaries. Wickedness, malignity and evil in thought and purpose is expressed by the Greek word, **poneria**. There is nothing good about these spirits. "Spiritual wickedness" could be translated from the Greek as "the spiritual things of wickedness." Every type of evil spirit is combined in this last category and all of them are wicked.

I do not believe it is necessary to name or to find out the name of these wicked spirits. If they are categorized, it is by the evil that they cause. They work to accomplish the direction of their superiors. There was only one time Jesus asked the name of the "unclean spirit" and he said his name was Legion, which only indicated that there were a great number of spirits possessing the men in the tombs (Matthew 8:28-34).

These four categories of spiritual forces – principalities, powers, rulers of darkness and wicked spirits – are the ranks of the Evil One's army. In order to stand against them, we must remember that our strength is not in ourselves, but comes from God through our Lord Jesus Christ. We stand in a place of victory, not defeat. That is how we must approach the struggle with the Evil One's army. He has already been defeated!

Now that we know the levels of the Evil One's army, we need to understand his strategy to distract and ultimately defeat the believer. When his strategy is no longer a secret, the believer can counter his tactics to be victorious rather than falling victim to his age-old tricks.

Chapter 4
STRATEGY OF THE EVIL ONE

Wise military leaders never go into battle without carefully studying the military strategy of their opponents. They need to be very familiar with how they operate, their character, their methods and tactics. To be effective in the spiritual battle, we must know our Enemy and his strategy.

Vagueness in teaching about the Evil One with no clear explanations of how to deal with him impedes Christians in living a victorious life in Christ. They do their best to live their lives for God but their Enemy remains undetected. The average Christian does not know who the Evil One is, or (even worse), does not believe he exists. This ignorance is the most powerful aspect of the Enemy's strategy – the secrecy of his methods.

To bring this statement to a better understanding, let's take a very brief look at United States history and the attack on Pearl Harbor on December 7, 1941. Lt. Commander Edwin T. Layton, the U.S. Pacific Fleet's intelligence officer was worried; although the Pacific command in Hawaii had determined that the Japanese were planning an attack, they did not know exactly where, when, how and with what weaponry. The Japanese navy had suddenly changed the radio call signs of its ships and the location of the Japanese aircraft carriers was unknown. The Communications Intelligence Unit at Pearl Harbor dismissed this as "irrelevant" because it was widely believed that the Japanese would attack in the Philippines or Thailand and that the Japanese planes and ships were inferior to American ones. The Japanese task force approached undetected to within 230 miles of Hawaii and struck a devastating blow to the naval base at Pearl Harbor. The surprise was complete.[17]

---

[17] Nathan Miller, *The Baltimore Sun,* Dec. 1, 1991, "Why was the Surprise Attack at Pearl Harbor Such a Surprise?"

Just as the secrecy of the strategy of the Japanese in World War II was instrumental in gaining a victory for them, so the Evil One uses this same ploy – he keeps his strategy secret. It follows that **the exposing of his strategy will be the beginning of the path to victory.**

We must define the terms we are using so that they are consistent. The first important term is strategy. Strategy is used in various areas of life: military, politics, business and even sports. Strategy is "a plan of action designed to achieve a particular goal."[18]

The Evil One has two main goals. The first and primary goal is to gain worship and glory for himself. This will be made clear during the end times when the Antichrist is set up to exercise worldwide dominion.

2 Thessalonians 2:3-4 ESV
Let no one deceive you in any way. For that day will not come, unless the rebellion comes first, and the man of lawlessness is revealed, the son of destruction,
who opposes and exalts himself against every so-called god or object of worship, so that he takes his seat in the temple of God, proclaiming himself to be God.

The second goal of the Evil One is to "steal, kill and destroy." Jesus describes him as a "thief" in the passage about the good shepherd.

John 10:10 KJV
The thief cometh not, but for to steal, and to kill, and to destroy: I am come that they might have life, and that they might have it more abundantly.

What is the difference between killing and destroying? At first, they appear to be synonymous. However, "kill" means "to sacrifice or slaughter," whereas "destroy" means to "put out of the way entirely,

---

[18] Wikipedia, "strategy"

abolish, put an end to, ruin, or render useless."[19] The emphasis in the latter is on ruin, annihilation and complete loss.

Since these are the goals, what is the strategy?

A strategy describes how the ends (goals) will be achieved by the means (resources). There are three parts to any strategy:

1. Devices (purposes)
2. Tactics (methods)
3. Implementation of resources

The Evil One uses these three components to accomplish his overall goals. The Bible uses specific words to parallel this strategy. The first component is devices, which are the purposes or plans.

2 Corinthians 2:11 KJV
Lest Satan should get an advantage of us: for we are not ignorant of his devices.

"Devices" is the Greek word **noema** and simply means, "that which thinks, the mind, thoughts or purposes." The devices are the specific purposes from the mind or thoughts. Thoughts will always devise a plan before any action is taken.

The second component of the strategy is the tactics utilized to accomplish the purposes. We described the word "tactics" from Aramaic in the chapter on *Suit Up and Stand* and noted that it always has an evil purpose. The Greek word used is also enlightening. It is **methodeia**, from which we get our English word, "method." It is a compound word that literally means, "with a road" or "on a road." The methods are the tactics of pursuit on a certain course that will accomplish the purpose. The word can mean crafty tricks or schemes. This is how it is used in Ephesians 4.

---

[19] *The New Thayer's Greek-English Lexicon*, p. 64.

Ephesians 4:14 NASB
As a result, we are no longer to be children, tossed here and there by
waves, and carried about by every wind of doctrine, by the trickery
of men, by craftiness in deceitful scheming [**methodeia**];

The methods that are pursued are implemented with certain weapons
or in a certain environment. This is the third part of the strategy. It is
the implementation of the methods with specific weapons.

A relevant business example is a company whose <u>purpose</u> is to sell
plasma donations to hospitals. The <u>methods</u> are the types of testing
employed to make sure the plasma is safe. The <u>implementation</u> and
resources are the lab, equipment and staff that accomplish the testing.
I learned recently of a company who had this purpose. Instead of
outsourcing the testing, the plasma company purchased the testing
company as a subsidiary so they could be sure that the testing was
being done correctly. They were controlling the implementation and
resources to make sure their overall purpose was accomplished.

A military example is the allocation of weapons to an area so that an
action can be effective. This would include the number of guns, tanks,
bombs, etc. needed to win the battle. The Greek word for weapons is
hoplon, and means "an instrument or implement."[20]

The record when Jesus was arrested in the garden provides a simple
example of the three parts of strategy. The purpose was to arrest him.
The tactic was to use Judas to betray him and the implementation was
to use soldiers with weapons to capture him.

John 18:3 KJV
Judas then, having received a band of men and officers from the chief
priests and Pharisees, cometh thither with lanterns and torches and
weapons [**hoplon**].

---

[20] Bullinger, *A Critical Lexicon and Concordance*, p. 861.

Now let's look at the following chart summarizing the Evil One's strategy. Each of the principalities has a specific part to play in the overall strategy. This chart is included here to introduce the following chapters which will show the specific piece of the armor that stands against each principality. The specific tactics will be explained in detail in these chapters. It would help you to mark this chart as a reference to be used while reading the central chapters of the book. The tactics are put in quotations to help you remember the Evil One's methods easily. They are like bookends that cover the range of the tactics.

Principalities	Devices (Purposes)	Tactics (Methods)	Implementation of Weapons
Beelzebub	Control, usurp the Lordship of Jesus Christ	"Dominate and poison"	Corrupt words, propaganda, false teaching
Devil	Slander, devour	"Cut and ensnare"	Accusation, guilt, rejection
Dragon	Divide, destroy	"Twist and separate"	Pride, offense, jealousy, stubbornness
Satan	Torment, oppress	"Shock and freeze"	Fear, sickness, catastrophes
Belial	Captivate, swallow	"Corrupt and distress"	Unworthiness, addictions, perversity
Serpent	Deceive, blind	"Dazzle and blind"	Counterfeit religion, lies, occult, witchcraft

Remember that the two main goals of the Evil One are to gain glory for himself and to ultimately destroy people, especially Christians. Let us begin to expose his devices and tactics even more so that they are no longer hidden in secret.

Chapter 5
OVERVIEW OF THE ARMOR OF VICTORY

Ephesians 6:10-17 APNT
From now on, my brothers, be strong in our Lord and in the immensity of his power
and put on the whole armor of God, so that you may be able to stand against the tactics of the Accuser,
because your struggle is not with flesh and blood, but with rulers and with authorities and with the possessors of this dark world and with the evil spirits that are under heaven.
Because of this, put on the whole armor of God, so that you will be able to engage the Evil [one] and, being prepared in everything, you will stand firm.
Therefore, stand and gird up your waist with truthfulness and put on the breastplate of justification
and bind [as a sandal] on your feet the preparation of the gospel of peace.
and with these, take to you the shield of faith, by which you will be empowered with strength to quench all the fiery arrows of the Evil [one].
and set on [your head] the helmet of redemption and take hold of the sword of the Spirit, which is the word of God.

In the chapter entitled *Our Spiritual Clothing*, we learned that putting on the armor is equivalent to putting on the Lord Jesus Christ. Each piece of the armor is parallel with these names: Lord, Jesus, and Christ. The designation of Lord means boss, master or guide. He leads the way as the "living Word" and is the "same yesterday and today and forever" (Hebrews 13:8 ESV). The name of Jesus means the deliverer and savior, who paid the price for our justification and redemption. The title of Christ is the Messiah or "anointed one" and shows the full measure of the gift of the Spirit that was on Jesus Christ.

The following chart introduces the six pieces of the armor of God and shows how they are arranged in an introversion. An introversion has sections which are similar in nature and complement one another, noted by A, B, and C.

		ACTION WE TAKE	PIECE OF ARMOR	SPIRITUAL CLOTHING	AGAINST PRINCI-PALITY
A	Lord/ Word	Gird your loins	belt	of truth (faithfulness)	Beelzebub
B	Jesus/ Blood	Put on	breastplate	of justification	Devil
C	Christ/ Spirit	Bind on	sandals	of the firm platform of the gospel of peace	Dragon
C	Christ/ Spirit	Raise up	shield	of the name of Jesus Christ	Satan
B	Jesus/ Blood	Set on your head	helmet	of redemption	Belial
A	Lord/ Word	Take hold of, clasp	sword	of the Spirit, the living Word	Serpent

The two A sections both have to do with the Word of God. The two B sections both have to do with what the blood of Jesus accomplished. Lastly, the two C sections have to do with the operation of the Spirit in our relationships in the body of Christ.

There is another way to understand how to put on the Lord, Jesus and Christ. It is the testimony of God regarding his Son and these three agree as a witness of the power of the gift God has given us.

1 John 5:5-9 NASB
And who is the one who overcomes the world, but he who believes that Jesus is the Son of God?

This is the one who came by water and blood, Jesus Christ; not with the water only, but with the water and with the blood.
And it is the Spirit who bears witness, because the Spirit is the truth. For there are three that bear witness, the Spirit and the water and the blood; and the three are in agreement.
If we receive the witness of men, the witness of God is greater; for the witness of God is this, that He has borne witness concerning His Son.

The water (of the Word), the living words of life (John 7:38), is the focus of the belt and the sword. The blood of Jesus is the focus of the breastplate and the helmet. The Spirit is the focus of the sandals and the shield.

One column of the chart contains the action we are responsible to take, followed by a column with what we put on: the pieces of the armor. The next column explains what the pieces represent in terms of our spiritual clothing. The last column is the principality that is counteracted by each piece of the armor.

This is the foundational overview of the next six chapters. Each chapter will explain one piece of the armor and its spiritual significance. The next section of each chapter will introduce the name of the specific principality and how it functions. The final section of each chapter will address the practical application of the piece of armor.

Chapter 6
THE BELT OF TRUTH

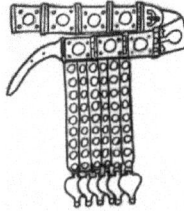

ACTION WE TAKE	PIECE OF ARMOR	SPIRITUAL CLOTHING	AGAINST PRINCIPALITY
Gird your loins	belt	of truth (faithfulness)	Beelzebub

The armor is not simply a set of helpful tips, but it is an impregnable defense against the Enemy when used properly. God chooses to begin describing this set of armor by talking about...a belt! Why, of all things, a belt?

The Roman soldier's belt or girdle was a piece of strong leather that was fastened around the waist. Leather or metal strips attached to the belt hung down and covered the lower half of the body to the knees. The belt secured the breastplate, keeping the armor in place, and supported the sword. That is why it is so important – it is the foundational piece that holds everything together. *Matthew Henry's Commentary* on Ephesians 6:14 states, "[truth] is the strength of our loins; and it girds [secures] on all other pieces of our armour, and therefore is first mentioned."

"Gird" means to "encompass about." To "gird on" something means "to get ready for war, make the source of your strength, or arm yourself with strength." David said that he was girded with God's strength.

THE BELT OF TRUTH

Psalm 18:32 KJV
It is God that girdeth me with strength, and maketh my way perfect.

"Gird up your loins" is an idiom used in the Hebrew culture to mean, "get ready for action." Since the people wore long flowing robes, when someone was going to run or do heavy work, they tucked the edges of their robes into a girdle so that they could move freely. Some English idioms that begin to capture the meaning are "roll up your sleeves," "brace your mind," or "get it together." Loins are the focus of the strength of the body (and also the location of the reproductive organs). The loins are the "seat of strength and vigour."[21]

The battlefield where we are engaged is in our minds. We are to gird up the loins of our minds. This idiom is used in the epistle of 1 Peter.

1 Peter 1:13 APNT
Because of this, gird up the loins of your thinking and be completely watchful and hope for the joy that will come to you at the appearing of our Lord Jesus Christ.

The mind consists of three parts: the will, thoughts or thinking, and the emotions. In each of these areas, we must base our strength on a reliable resource outside of ourselves. The extent of our strength will depend on what we choose as the resource.

Gird up your loins with (make the source of your strength) "truth." When we read that we are to gird our minds with "truth," we should immediately think of God's Word, the word of truth. But why can we rely on God's Word to always be the truth? The particular word for truth in Aramaic is **qushta** and comes from a root verb that means "to shoot straight as an arrow" (hit the bull's eye). It has to do with God's truthfulness, uprightness, total reliability, stability, faithfulness and integrity.

---

[21] *The New Brown-Driver-Briggs-Gesenius Hebrew and English Lexicon*, p. 323.

The use of the word "truth" meaning truthfulness or faithfulness is corroborated in the Old Testament. The Greek word used in Ephesians 6:14 is **aletheia** and the following use of **aletheia** in the Septuagint further unfolds the meaning of truth as part of the armor. Isaiah 11:5 is a prophecy about the Branch (Jesus Christ) that would come out of the house of Jesse, that he would be mighty in spirit and wisdom and righteousness.

Isaiah 11:5 ESV
Righteousness shall be the belt of his waist, and faithfulness [**aletheia**] *the belt of his loins.*

Jesus Christ fulfilled this prophecy by relying upon God's faithfulness to his Word and to all his promises as the source of his strength. Jesus literally believed that every one of God's prophecies regarding him would come to pass. As he studied passages such as Psalm 22 and Isaiah 53 in his youth, the records about his suffering became clear to him. Later, when he actually went through the torture of the cross, the words he had embedded in his heart and mind gave him the strength to complete his unique task of redeeming mankind from sin.

"Truth," as a piece of the armor that God has given to us, is about God's utter reliability and integrity and faithfulness. "Gird up your loins with truth" means to draw your strength from the absolute faithfulness and reliability of God and his Word.

The "truth" referred to here is the very character and nature of God himself. We trust in God's Word because God is totally reliable and his words are faithful. People change, but God does not change. We can absolutely base our lives and decisions on the integrity inherent in his Word. God is not a man that he should lie (Numbers 23:19). His Word is always straight on the target, never veering off in another direction. We sometimes veer from the target, and as a result we have no strength. We must make God's absolute reliability and truthfulness the source of our strength.

Here are a few records that declare God's truthfulness and integrity:

49

Deuteronomy 7:9 KJV
Know therefore that the LORD thy God, he is God, the faithful God, which keepeth covenant and mercy with them that love him and keep his commandments to a thousand generations;

Numbers 23:19-20 KJV
God is not a man, that he should lie; neither the son of man, that he should repent: hath he said, and shall he not do it? or hath he spoken, and shall he not make it good?
Behold, I have received commandment to bless: and he hath blessed: and I cannot reverse it.

Malachi 3:6 KJV
For I am the LORD, I change not; therefore ye sons of Jacob are not consumed.

2 Thessalonians 3:3 APNT
But the LORD is faithful, who will keep you and rescue you from the Evil [one].

1 Corinthians 1:9-10 AMP
God is faithful, reliable, trustworthy, and therefore ever true to His promise, and He can be depended on; By Him you were called into companionship and participation with His Son, Jesus Christ our Lord.

God's Word in our minds gives us stability; it is unchanging truth. His Word always means exactly what it says. His promises never change, even though our experiences with people and circumstances may teach us the opposite. Since God never changes, when we choose to believe his Word, we are enabled to focus clearly on his truth.

2 Corinthians 1:20 APNT
For all the promises of God in him, in Christ, are yes. Because of this by way of him, we give an "Amen" to the glory of God.

Steve Myers of the United Church of God has a great article called, "Guard the Door to your Mind." He compares our minds to our own personal computers. In order to keep the computer safe from malicious attacks, we must install a piece of software called a firewall. We also put in anti-virus software that finds and deletes harmful programs. We do this to make sure that spyware or malware will be detected and immediately deleted or quarantined before it can harm the computer's operating system. We take special care not to download unfamiliar software or open suspicious emails, even if they have interesting headlines.[22] If we guard our computers so carefully, what about our minds? In like manner, we should install a spiritual firewall in our minds to guard against detrimental thoughts.

God's Word is truth. It flies straight as an arrow and hits the target every time. It is backed up by all that God is, so it has greater authority than words from any other source. Therefore, we gird up the loins of our minds by replacing poison words that come from a multitude of sources with the powerful and faithful words of God. We counteract the incessant lies of the Enemy that bombard us by speaking the dominating truth from God that sustains us and is the source of our strength.

Which words do we believe? The words of men or the words from God? Words have great power, both for good and for evil. Words can be edifying, but also they can be poison arrows that inflict mortal wounds and eventually lead to death.

Proverbs 18:21 KJV
Death and life are in the power of the tongue: and they that love it shall eat the fruit thereof.

In summary, the meaning of "gird up yours loins with truth" is to make the faithfulness and integrity of God's Word the source of your strength. This is why this piece of the armor is the defense against attacks from the principality of Beelzebub, who attacks with words.

---

[22] www.ucg.org/united-new/guard-the-door-to-your-mind

PRINCIPALITY OF BEELZEBUB

The name Beelzebub can be difficult to comprehend but the New Testament gives the following information.

Matthew 12:24 KJV
But when the Pharisees heard it, they said, This fellow doth not cast out devils, but by Beelzebub the prince of the devils.

In this verse, he is called the prince of the devils. "Prince" has the same root word in Greek as "principality." It should read "a prince" of demons, not "the prince" since Beelzebub is not the only principality. In Jennings *Lexicon of the Syriac New Testament*, he suggests that "Beelzebub" is possibly a corruption of the Aramaic word **beldabba,** which means "enemy," and is literally, "the master of slander" or "lord of words."[23] Beelzebub's primary tactic is to use words to dominate and control people.

"Beelzebub" (also spelled Baalzebub) is the name of a Philistine god worshipped at Ekron. His name means "lord of the flies" and it was assumed by the Philistines that he was a god who could cause or cure diseases.[24] King Ahaziah sent messengers to inquire of this god to see if he would recover from a sickness he was suffering from.

2 Kings 1:2-3 KJV
And Ahaziah fell down through a lattice in his upper chamber that was in Samaria, and was sick: and he sent messengers, and said unto them, Go, enquire of Baalzebub the god of Ekron whether I shall recover of this disease.
But the angel of the LORD said to Elijah the Tishbite, Arise, go up to meet the messengers of the king of Samaria, and say unto them, Is it not because there is not a God in Israel, that ye go to enquire of Baalzebub the god of Ekron?

---

[23] William Jennings, *Lexicon to the Syriac New Testament,* p. 39.
[24] *Dictionary of Demons and Deities in the Bible,* p. 154.

The first part of Beelzebub's name is "Baal" which means "Lord." Baal was the god of nature, controlling the weather, fertility, and crops. Although his characteristics were not clearly defined, he was considered to be very much like Yahweh, the true LORD. This is very possibly why Israel was instructed to destroy the Canaanite nations that were worshipping Baal and Ashtoreth. Israel often confused the worship of Yahweh with the worship of Baal; in spite of being frequently corrected by the prophets, they continually reverted to setting up groves to contain their idols. Jezebel, the wife of King Ahab, tried to totally replace the worship of Yahweh with Baal worship during the time of the prophet Elijah.

Beelzebub sets up dominions or lordships. There are lords or "baals," if you will, that concentrate in specific geographical areas. There were many Baals in local areas of the land of Canaan: Baal-Berith, Baal-Peor, Baal-Hermon, etc. The reason there were so many local Baals is that each local city wanted to have its own "territorial god." Baal was also the god of the Phoenicians.

This is similar to today's world where a given city or region may have established strongholds, certain types of customs or ideologies. For example, in Sedona, Arizona, there is a strong belief in new age concepts such as tarot cards, the vortex, astral worship and the like. Another example is San Francisco where various sexual spirits are concentrated and have instituted a strong cultural influence. Though today we do not worship idols such as the Baals in groves, the concentration of certain spirits in local areas is how the principality of Beelzebub dominates cities and also larger areas of the world.

Some Bible teachers call the spiritual rulers "territorial spirits."[25] But the best explanation is that they are strongholds of beliefs ruled over by a concentration of certain kinds of devil spirits. These end up having "lordship" over the people, and the community mindset is a very powerful influence over people who live in these areas.

---

[25] Peter Wagner, *Dark Angels*, p. 77.

Principality	Devices (Purposes)	Tactics (Methods)	Weapons
Beelzebub	Control, usurp the Lordship of Jesus Christ	"Dominate and poison"	Corrupt words, propaganda, false teaching

Beelzebub, or **Beldabba**, is the lord or master of words. His second major tactic is to use words to defeat and weaken the believer by having them believe his words instead of God's Word. He is an Enemy whose words are the complete opposite of God's words. He influences good people to use poison words and to think there is nothing wrong. He also uses words to influence people to distrust the faithfulness of God. Believing these words is like drinking a deadly poison.

Mark 16:18 APNT
And they will capture snakes, and if they should drink a deadly poison, it will harm not them and they will place their hands on the sick and they will be made whole.

The word "poison" in this verse is referring to words. "Snakes" is not the normal word for serpent. In Aramaic it comes from the verb "to show" and could be translated "pretenders." I believe that it refers here to the principality of Beelzebub and his minions. "Capture" is literally "to take," but in war it is translated "capture." The "deadly poison," or literally, the poison of death, is the figure of speech, *hypocatastasis*, calling words poison. Here is just one verse that corroborates the use of this figure.

Psalm 140:3 NASB
They sharpen their tongues as a serpent; poison of a viper is under their lips. Selah.

Most of the time Beelzebub uses someone in authority to perpetrate his poison words. His main purpose is to control people, especially Christians, and to usurp the Lordship of Jesus Christ in their lives.

His tactics are to "dominate and poison." He uses the weapon of propaganda to take over areas of culture – such as music, education, and politics – to promote his lies. He even uses false teaching in the Church to diminish the position of the Lord Jesus Christ and elevate men instead.

PRACTICAL APPLICATION

In practical application, putting on the belt of truth involves our response to the attacks that come from the principality of Beelzebub using the authority of men's words. We counteract poison words with the words of truth from God's Word that apply. Because God's words are stronger than the poison, it effectively neutralizes the effect of the poison. Here are just a few examples:

Doctors: "You have terminal cancer."

God: "I am the Lord that healeth thee." (Exodus 16:26)
"...by whose stripes [wounds] you were healed." (1 Peter 3:7)

Parents: "You'll never amount to anything."

God: "Now unto him that is able to do exceeding abundantly above all that we ask or think according to the power that worketh in us." (Ephesians 3:20)

Media: "The housing, bond and stock market are failing and you will lose all your money."

God: "And I will rebuke the devourer for your sakes, and he shall not destroy the fruits of your ground; neither shall your vine cast her fruit before the time in the field, saith the LORD of hosts. And all nations shall call you blessed: for ye shall be a delightsome land, saith the LORD of hosts." (Malachi 3:11-12)

What is the part of the Lord Jesus Christ that we gird on? It is the truth that Jesus is the only true Lord! Anything we put ahead of him is another lord (small "l") and could eventually become a stronghold or lordship in our lives. For example, the desire for wealth and riches is not necessarily evil of itself, but combined with the influence of the stronghold of materialism could lead to various detrimental activities like working 80 hours a week at our jobs, going into unnecessary debt, being unable to make necessary payments, etc. Eventually we begin comparing ourselves to others, and making poor decisions which affect our families and our relationships within the body of Christ. Something else besides Jesus Christ has become lord.

Another example is in the area of medicine. Our culture has a high regard for the medical profession. My own father was a chest surgeon and there were also other doctors in my family. Consequently, I grew up with much admiration for the medical field. In fact, both my father and my grandfather helped many people during the course of their careers. But both of these men knew that even though they had a lot of education, it was God who was the healer, not them. Because of the concentration of the lordships of Beelzebub in this field, there has been a substitution of the lordship of medicine over the healing power of Jesus Christ. It is obvious for example, when a person is sick, one of the first questions that are asked by others is, "What did the doctor say?" The doctor is not a Lord with a capital L. That is why "poison words" of the doctors, oftentimes spoken in ignorance or arrogance, have so much power.

We need to strengthen our minds with the truth of God's Word in order to stand against the "Baals" of our culture. We don't normally think of these things mentioned as spiritually bad, but if we renamed the city referred to earlier as Baal-San Francisco, then it would be more obvious what we need to stand against. Often, someone from another city or area can see very easily what we do not see living in our own city or state. When I first moved with my family in 1965 to Waterloo, Iowa, I was shocked to find out that a river divided the east and west sides of the city. One side was occupied by blacks and the other by whites. If you were one or the other, you didn't go on the other side. I had grown up with mixed races up until that time and it did not even occur to me to be prejudiced. However, that was not the case in that city. We need to help each other identify the lordships that are strongly concentrated in our schools, neighborhoods, towns, cities and states. Then we will be able to stand together against these cultural and local lordships.

A Biblical example tells us what we need to do to stand against Beelzebub and his evil helpers. In Ephesus, where the goddess Diana was worshipped and revered, the silversmiths had major control of the trade in that area. After Paul arrived and people began giving up their idols, the silversmiths complained:

Acts 19:27 KJV
So that not only this our craft is in danger to be set at nought; but also that the temple of the great goddess Diana should be despised, and her magnificence should be destroyed, whom all Asia and the world worshippeth.

What changed Ephesus was the introduction of the light of TRUTH, bringing deliverance for many people from using magic arts and witchcraft.

Acts 19:18-20 KJV
And many that believed came, and confessed, and shewed their deeds. Many of them also which used curious arts brought their books together, and burned them before all men: and they counted the price of them, and found it fifty thousand pieces of silver.
So mightily grew the word of God and prevailed.

The light cast out the darkness so effectively that "all they which dwelt in Asia heard the word of the Lord Jesus, both Jews and Greeks" (Acts 19:10).

In this same way, we can gird up the loins of our minds with truth. We have to cast down the things that are lords in our lives and bring everything in line with the truth of what God says in his Word. We need to continually ask the question, "What words are you basing your decisions on?"

An example in my own life came when I was puzzling over why I did not have prosperity in my life even though I had been tithing for years. Over a year of diligent study regarding giving and prosperity, God showed me that I had developed a belief during my childhood that life would always be a struggle financially. The light of the faithful promises of God's Word (such as 2 Corinthians 9:8-12 and Philippians 4:19) dispelled this strong belief and enabled me to be delivered in this area. I continue to specifically apply these verses whenever I am tempted to be worried financially.

The belt of the faithfulness of God's Word encompasses our thoughts and reasonings. We need to compare each thought with the pertinent truth from God's Word and then decide which is right, our thoughts or HIS. We need to answer the question of who or what is Lord in our lives. We must make the source of our strength God's integrity and faithfulness to all his promises.

Hebrews 10:23 AMP
Let us seize and hold tightly the confession of our hope without wavering, for He who promised is reliable and trustworthy and faithful [to His word];

Chapter 7
THE BREASTPLATE OF JUSTIFICATION

ACTION WE TAKE	PIECE OF ARMOR	SPIRITUAL CLOTHING	AGAINST PRINCIPALITY
Put on	breastplate	of justification	Devil

The breastplate covered the soldier's heart and chest area. It was usually made of woven metal or coarse heavy cloth so that it would provide protection for the upper body, especially the heart and lungs. It was a crucial piece of the armor because a chest exposed to attack could mean death. In Latin, it was called the **lorica segmenta**, because it was made from adjoining pieces of metal.

Regarding this piece of the armor, some have taught that the breastplate is worn only on the front, but this has proven to be untrue after studying the actual piece of Roman armor. The Roman breastplate covered both back and front. If the back was exposed, the heart could be pierced by arrows coming from that direction. As believers, we need this breastplate to cover our whole torso and to protect our hearts.

The word "heart" as used in the Bible represents a person's will, mind and emotions; it is equivalent to how we use the word "mind." This is the area that the Devil or the Accuser comes to attack via thoughts and whispers. The purpose of the breastplate is to deflect his accusations so they become ineffective and useless, as blows glance off the armor.

The breastplate is our justification in Aramaic and it becomes clear why when we understand exactly what justification is. There are two words for "righteousness" in Aramaic, but there is only one in Greek. The distinction between the two words helps us to understand several key passages about righteousness, especially in Romans. The first word for righteousness is **kanutha** and means "uprightness" and has to do with having a new nature. When we believe that God raised Jesus from the dead, we receive a new nature that is "right." It is accounted to us because Jesus paid the price for Adam's sin in his death by offering himself as the payment for mankind's sin nature. This new nature is perfect and upright in God's sight; he esteems us righteous just as though we had died with him (Romans 6:7-8). Our sins have been declared utterly dead.

The second Aramaic word for righteousness is **zadiqutha** and is translated "justification." An easy way to understand it is by noting the underlying verb action. It means "to be brought up to a standard." God has an immutable standard of moral and ethical justice that is unreachable by man's most gallant efforts. This righteousness could not be attained by keeping the Law because no man born with a sin nature was able to keep the Law. Jesus, who was born free from a sin nature, fulfilled every precept of the Law. The justification that Jesus received can now be legally transferred to any person who believes on him and makes him Lord. His resurrection from the dead was overwhelming proof that the righteous requirements of the God's Law had been met. When Jesus rose from the dead, we rose with him, completely justified. **He rose in order to justify us, to bring us up to God's standard.**

Romans 4 shows the two Aramaic words for righteousness and the context is about God reckoning righteousness to Abraham.

Romans 4:23-5:2 APNT
And not on his behalf only was this written: HIS FAITH WAS COUNTED FOR UPRIGHTNESS,
but also on our behalf, because he is also prepared to count [uprightness to] those who believe in him who raised our Lord Jesus Christ from the dead,

who was delivered up for our sins and rose in order to justify us.
Therefore, because we are justified by faith, we have peace toward
God by our Lord Jesus Christ,
by whom we were brought by faith to this grace in which we stand
and boast in the hope of the glory of God.

Justification is a legal requirement in order for us to have access to God at any time. We have been legally acquitted from blame, therefore we can come directly into God's presence with peace. This justification is the foundation for all of the rights given to us in Christ. Without being legally acquitted, we could not have been redeemed, reconciled to God, sanctified, forgiven of our sins or given any other privileges that now belong to us as sons of God. We have access to the throne room of God's grace!

Ephesians 3:12 ESV
in whom we have boldness and access with confidence through our
faith in him.

The Old Testament also sheds light on the meaning of the breastplate. When God ordained Aaron to be a priest to the people of Israel in the wilderness, he designed a breastplate to be worn on the ephod of Aaron's garment. This breastplate was made of metal and contained twelve precious stones, three in each of four rows. Each stone represented one of the tribes of Israel. Each year, when the high priest went into the Holy of Holies to make atonement for the sins of the people, he carried a representation of all Israel on the breastplate that was situated over his heart. This was called the "breastplate of judgment" (Exodus 28:15). Once the high priest offered the sacrifice of atonement, the people were judged righteous before God.

Hebrews 9:24-26 KJV
For Christ is not entered into the holy places made with hands, which
are the figures of the true; but into heaven itself, now to appear in the
presence of God for us:
Nor yet that he should offer himself often, as the high priest entereth
into the holy place every year with blood of others;

THE BREASTPLATE OF JUSTIFICATION

For then must he often have suffered since the foundation of the world: but now once in the end of the world hath he appeared to put away sin by the sacrifice of himself.

Jesus Christ is the great high priest who entered the Holy of Holies once for all and made atonement for the sins of all people. He accomplished this by his death, which paid the penalty for all sin. Sin separated man from God, but Jesus Christ conquered sin. Once sin had been carried away by Jesus, God dramatically tore the veil that separated the Holy of Holies from top to bottom, giving his people free access into his presence. Ephesians 2:18 says, "for through him we both have access by one Spirit unto the Father." This access is the result of what we have been given in God's marvelous gift. God had a wonderful purpose for providing us with remission of sins and justification. He desired an intimate relationship with us and a way to pour out his love.

Romans 8:31-33 says, "If God be for us, who can be against us? He that spared not his own Son, but delivered him up for us all, how shall he not with him also freely give us all things? Who shall lay anything to the charge of God's elect? It is God that justifieth." God has declared us justified, which gives us complete access to him. Nothing can separate us from the love of God in Christ. When we cry, "Abba, our Father," God hears our cry. We no longer need to accept any kind of condemnation or accusation. All rips, jabs, and accusations directed toward us are deflected by the breastplate signifying our justification. It is important for us to remember that we have this justification not because we were good – because clearly, we were not – but rather because Jesus was obedient and loving enough to attain it for us!

The breastplate of justification covers the heart and protects the torso. This is the same breastplate that is described in the Old Testament in a prophecy regarding Jesus Christ.

Isaiah 59:17 ESV
He put on righteousness [**tzedaqah** – the Hebrew equivalent of **zadiqutha**] *as a breastplate, and a helmet of salvation on his head;*

62

he put on garments of vengeance for clothing, and wrapped himself in zeal as a cloak.

The belt and breastplate work together to cover the entire torso. The belt covers the lower loins, the center of strength for the body; it secures the breastplate and holds the front and back together. The breastplate protects the heart. By the blood of Jesus Christ, God has given us access to himself, acquittal from blame, and continued forgiveness and cleansing of our sins.

PRINCIPALITY OF THE DEVIL

The "Devil" is a common term applied to the Evil One. "Devil" is the same name as "Accuser." In Aramaic, the word **akelqartza** is the term for Devil, meaning literally, "eater of pieces." The idiom paints the picture of a person being a piece of bread that is broken and torn in pieces and then eaten by the Devil.

The Greek word for "devil" is **diabolos** and is a compound word comprised of **dia,** meaning "through" and **ballo,** meaning "to throw something." Literally the word **diabalos** describes "the repetitive action of hitting something again, again, again, again, until finally the wall or membrane is so worn down that it can be completely and thoroughly penetrated."[26] It is like pounding the cover of a wooden box so many times that it finally caves in. Both the Aramaic and Greek terms are very vivid pictures of accusation.

The Devil is an accuser. To "accuse" means "to charge someone with an offense." This principality's primary purpose is to slander. Slander is defined as "a false accusation of an offense or a malicious misrepresentation of someone's words or actions."[27]

Another definition of "devil" is "devourer." The Devil uses words to cut or bite a person.

---

[26] Rick Renner, *Spiritual Weapons to Defeat the Enemy*, p. 31.
[27] Vocabulary.com, "slander"

Proverbs 30:14
There is a generation, whose teeth are as swords, and their jaw teeth
as knives, to devour the poor from off the earth, and the needy from
among men.

The Scribes and Pharisees endeavored to devour Jesus with their
accusations.

Luke 11:53-12:1 APNT
And while he was speaking these [things] to them, the scribes and
Pharisees began to be offended and they grew angry and were
criticizing his words.
And they were plotting against him in many [ways], seeking to catch
something from his mouth in order to be able to accuse [literally eat]
him.

Galatians 5:15 KJV
Now if you bite and devour one another, be careful that you are not
devoured by one another.

The Greek word for "bite" here is **dakno**. It is used metaphorically
and means "to wound the soul, cut, lacerate, rend with reproaches."[28]
This verse from Galatians is a figure of speech, comparing the
wounds from biting speech to the tearing and consuming of a wild
animal such as a wolf or bear.

The Devil's tactic is to use words to cut or tear a person apart and
afterwards, to ensnare him.

Principality	Devices (Purposes)	Tactics (Methods)	Weapons
Devil	Slander, devour	"Cut and ensnare"	Accusation, guilt, rejection

The snare is the second half of the Devil's tactic, or the other
bookend.

---

[28] *The New Thayer's Greek English Lexicon*, p. 124.

2 Timothy 2:26 ESV
And they may come to their senses and escape from the snare of the
devil, after being captured by him to do his will.

The snare spoken of here is to do the Devil's will and it keeps the
person trapped and in anguish. One of the weapons used to implement
this tactic is guilt for past sins. The cutting aspect of the attack is the
use of words, for example: "How dare you think you could lead God's
people? You have committed a horrendous sin!" Unable to shake the
weight of the guilt and condemnation can cause a person to fail to
receive God's love and forgiveness. Putting on the breastplate of
justification will deflect the accusing words of the Enemy and free
the person from the trap in which they would otherwise be hopelessly
ensnared.

PRACTICAL APPLICATION

An accusation can come from within (our own thoughts) or from an
outside source (someone else's words), both of which can be
devastating. The accusations that come from our own thoughts are
words that the Evil One has introduced into our minds and we have
believed. We may think these thoughts are genuinely our own and
that they must be true simply because we are thinking them. Other
accusations come from someone else pointing out our faults or
failures. Regardless of the source of the accusations, we must put on
the breastplate of justification.

Faultfinding is rampant in the Church. After an uplifting teaching and
heartfelt service, it is not surprising that the Devil immediately tries
to negate the positive effect of the Word. He sends someone, perhaps
with good intentions to remind the teacher or pastor of an important
point he left out, something "wrong" he said, a verse he didn't quote
correctly or something like that. The temptation is to be discouraged,
because the pastor is aware of his own faults. It is important to repent
of any true fault, but it is also important to recognize that even if an
accusation is true to some degree, the breastplate must be kept on.

Our justification is not of ourselves, but because of our identity in Christ. We can receive criticism, but not be devastated by it. We can use our free-from-blame access to talk over the situation with God.

I had a vision many years ago which really helped me in this area. The Roman breastplate is made of metal, but the "Christ in you" breastplate was made of very strong material which does not exist as far as I know. In the vision, it was transparent, impenetrable and molded to cover every square inch of the upper body. Usually impenetrable material is rather stiff, like the suit of the Marvel comic super hero Iron Man. This material was very light. It was transparent so that people could still see my heart and love shining through, but could not penetrate it with accusations. The breastplate of justification guards our hearts from accusations devastating our lives. It molds to cover all the areas of the heart and mind, so there is nothing that it cannot protect. That's the kind of breastplate we have in Jesus Christ!

The answer to someone accusing us from the outside is to give the situation to the Lord to handle. Even Michael the archangel did this. He was disputing with the Devil about the body of Moses.

Jude 1:9 APNT
Now Michael, the archangel, who, when he was debating with the Accuser, spoke about the body of Moses, did not dare to bring on him the judgment of blasphemy, but said, "The LORD will rebuke you."

When we are involved in situations where we are being accused of wrongdoing, we must allow God to judge the situation and do the rebuking necessary. Then we will deflect the Accuser's attempt to cut and ensnare us.

Divorce is an area where many accusations are exchanged between embittered parties. Often one of the spouses involved feels that if only he or she had behaved differently, the divorce would not have happened. If not squelched, this pattern of self-accusation can turn into an inability to receive love from a new partner. The snare would be unforgiveness of self and sometimes bitterness. The person in this situation would be challenged to believe that God has cleansed and forgiven their sins. The key is to remember that justification comes from Christ and not from anything a person can do to earn it. It does not matter whether a person is right or wrong in his own eyes. No one deserves justification from God. Every believer has been made accepted in Christ through forgiveness of ALL sins, by grace.

Ephesians 1:6-7 KJV
To the praise of the glory of his grace, wherein he hath made us accepted in the beloved.
In whom we have redemption through his blood, the forgiveness of sins, according to the riches of his grace;

Sometimes we face accusation when there is actual wrongdoing on our part. Then the cutting has to do with believing that the sin is too bad for God to forgive. The blood of Jesus Christ cleanses us from or washes away all sin (1 John 1:7). When we have sinned we need to receive reproof, even if only from God himself, and repent (turn back the opposite way). The snare would be to wallow in self-pity or condemnation and not receive God's cleansing and restoration. Again, justification is not earned, but given because of the work of our Lord Jesus Christ.

An actual example of how to put on the breastplate of justification is in the record of Jesus' temptation in the wilderness. The first accusation aimed at him from the Devil is couched in a question regarding his relationship to God. At his baptism, he had just heard the voice of God calling him "my beloved Son."

Luke 4:2-4 KJV
Being forty days tempted of the devil. And in those days he did eat nothing: and when they were ended, he afterward hungered.
And the devil said unto him, If thou be the Son of God, command this stone that it be made bread.
And Jesus answered him, saying, It is written, That man shall not live by bread alone, but by every word of God.
It is important to note that Jesus had been in the wilderness for forty days and had eaten nothing during that time. Accusations tend to

affect us more when we are in a weakened state either physically, mentally or spiritually. The Accuser (Devil) tempted Jesus by asking, "Are you really the son of God?" He whispered, "If so, then use your own power to provide for your physical needs." Rather than take the bait by answering the question, Jesus refuted the temptation to provide for his own needs with a quotation from Deuteronomy. The context of this verse is the time during the 40 years in the wilderness when Israel lived on manna, which was totally provided by God.

Deuteronomy 8:3 ESV
And he humbled you and let you hunger and fed you with manna, which you did not know, nor did your fathers know, that he might make you know that man does not live by bread alone, but man lives by every word that comes from the mouth of the LORD.

The Aramaic Peshitta text in Luke 4:4 for "word" is a different noun and is translated as "answer." This verse was the answer that God gave Jesus to remember and quote back to the Accuser. It was as though he put on the breastplate of justification and stated unequivocally that God would provide his needs in every category BECAUSE he was indeed the son of God!

In summary, when accusations come our way (either from ourselves or others), immediately check to see if the breastplate is firmly in place. Repent if needed, but then immediately seek your intimate relationship with God again. Be loved by him and enjoy his tender forgiveness. Do not question IF you are a son of God. You are! God has declared that we are justified, which gives us complete access to him. Nothing can separate us from the love of God in Christ.

Chapter 8
THE SANDALS OF THE GOSPEL OF PEACE

ACTION WE TAKE	PIECE OF ARMOR	SPIRITUAL CLOTHING	AGAINST PRINCIPALITY
Bind on	sandals	of the firm platform of the gospel of peace	Dragon

In this chapter we will investigate the part of the armor that has to do with the feet. The sandals of a Roman soldier, called **caligae**, were made of tough leather laced tightly on the foot. The soles had sharp nails attached to them that were intended to give the soldier superior traction on slippery ground. These nails were also used offensively to wound an opponent. During a battle, greaves of metal were attached to the sandals in order to protect the soldier's legs against lacerations. The greaves also aided the soldier as he walked through the dangerous terrain often encountered on the battlefield. The greaves were laced up the ankles and provided support for the calf and leg. The combination of sandal and greave gave the soldier a firm platform to stand upon when fighting in battle.

We are to figuratively bind studded sandals like these on our own feet. What do the sandals represent spiritually? The "preparation of the gospel of peace" in Ephesians 6:15 is difficult to understand, and is therefore probably the most misunderstood part of the armor. We need to remember that every part of the armor has to do with the power base we have in our Lord Jesus Christ. The verse becomes easy to understand when we understand the meaning of the word "preparation."

In Greek, "preparation" is the word **en hetoimasia** which comes from the root word meaning "to be ready, to prepare." It can be translated "preparation" but also "a prepared foundation or base." Here the emphasis is on the platform one is standing upon rather than on being ready for action. It could perhaps be better translated as "a sure foothold."[29] The New American Standard Version of Ephesians 2:10 says "For we are His workmanship, created in Christ Jesus for good works, which God prepared beforehand, that we should walk in them." God has prepared the works for us. In order to accomplish these works, we need to put on our sandals to give us a sure foothold for walking in those works.

The sure platform on which the soldier stands is the gospel of peace. "Of" here is used as a genitive of relation and means "the gospel which brings peace." This gospel is the good news of Christ and that all believers are called to be one in Christ.

Romans 1:16 KJV
For I am not ashamed of the gospel of Christ: for it is the power of God unto salvation to every one that believeth; to the Jew first, and also to the Greek.

The gospel is the power of God for salvation! This good news was a mystery in other ages, but was revealed to the apostle Paul.

Ephesians 3:3-6 KJV
How that by revelation he made known unto me the mystery; (as I wrote afore in few words,
Whereby, when ye read, ye may understand my knowledge in the mystery of Christ)

---

[29] *The Expositor's Bible Commentary*, p. 88.

Which in other ages was not made known unto the sons of men, as it is now revealed unto his holy apostles and prophets by the Spirit; That the Gentiles should be fellowheirs, and of the same body, and partakers of his promise in Christ by the gospel:

The mystery revealed to Paul is that every member of the body of Christ is special and has a function to perform (1 Corinthians 12:27). No person in the body is without purpose, and each one is set in exactly the place that God has determined is the best place. Each member of the body of Christ is vital to the proper functioning of the entire body, and no member is insignificant or trivial.

The good news of the body of Christ eradicates all the separations the world imposes between people – Jew versus Gentile, male versus female, young versus old, rich versus poor, etc. In the first century the biggest barrier was between the Jews and Gentiles, but actually all the walls between all people have been broken down.

Ephesians 2:14 NLT
For Christ himself has brought peace to us. He united Jews and Gentiles into one people when, in his own body on the cross, he broke down the wall of hostility that separated us.

The whole body is "fitly joined together," and the way the body of Christ is designed provides a bond of peace between each of the members (Ephesians 4:3). The head of the body is Christ. The head energizes the whole body to build itself up in love. This brings peace for each member.

Ephesians 4:16 NLT
He makes the whole body fit together perfectly. As each part does its own special work, it helps the other parts grow, so that the whole body is healthy and growing and full of love.

The gospel of peace is our firm platform as we stand against the principality of the Dragon.

PRINCIPALITY OF THE DRAGON

The Dragon is the principality whose main purpose is to cause divisions and destruction. His primary weapon is pride.

"Dragon" is the Hebrew word, **tanniyn**, and can mean "sea monster" or "dragon." The uses of the word "dragon" in the Old Testament indicate that it could be a land monster or sea monster. Its form is similar to a serpent, but includes feet and sometimes multiple heads.[30] The Dragon is closely allied with another monster called Leviathan, and is called both a fleeing serpent and twisting serpent.

Isaiah 27:1 ESV
In that day the LORD with his hard and great and strong sword will punish Leviathan the fleeing serpent, Leviathan the twisting serpent, and he will slay the dragon that is in the sea.

In the book of Job, there is an ongoing debate between Job and his friends about what caused all the catastrophes in Job's life. His friends were adamant that Job must have done something wrong for so much evil to befall him. Yet, Job declared that he was righteous. Finally, God stepped in and asked Job some very pointed questions about where his righteousness had come from. God's questions unveiled Job's pride in his own righteousness. As God spoke to Job, he gave him an entire discourse (in chapter 41) regarding Leviathan and his description.

Job 41:1-8 ESV
Can you draw out Leviathan with a fishhook or press down his tongue with a cord?
Can you put a rope in his nose or pierce his jaw with a hook?
Will he make many pleas to you? Will he speak to you soft words?
Will he make a covenant with you to take him for your servant forever?

---

[30] *Dictionary of Deities and Demons in the Bible*, p. 266.

Will you play with him as with a bird, or will you put him on a leash for your girls?
Will traders bargain over him? Will they divide him up among the merchants?
Can you fill his skin with harpoons or his head with fishing spears?
Lay your hands on him; remember the battle – you will not do it again!

God uses the sea monster, Leviathan, to reveal to Job that his problem is pride. As God reveals the monster, the depiction of Leviathan highlights that he is the ruler of pride.

Job 41:34 ESV
He sees everything that is high; he is king over all the sons of pride.

The International Standard Version translates verse 34 as, "He looks down on everything that is high; he rules over every kind of pride." Pride and Leviathan are practically synonymous. It is hard to separate them.

Job 41:15 KJV
His scales are his pride, shut up together as with a close seal.

Leviathan's arrogance and haughtiness stems from the tight-sealed scales covering his body. His scales are so close together that no air can come between them. They are joined one to the other and cannot be pulled apart. People that are prideful become stubborn; just as the scales or folds of Leviathan's flesh, they are impenetrable, firm in themselves and unable to be moved. These people refuse to be told anything.

Another characteristic of Leviathan is that he is stiff-necked.

Job 41:22 NLT
The tremendous strength in Leviathan's neck strikes terror wherever it goes.

The "neck" refers to the human will. The person with a stiff-necked posture has a prideful appearance. Stiff-necked pride and stubbornness are an accurate description of Leviathan. This stiff-necked, prideful attitude was attributed to Israel as they wandered in the wilderness for 40 years (Acts 7:51).

Job 41:24 KJV
His heart is as firm as a stone; yea, as hard as a piece of the nether millstone.

An extremely stubborn person could be described like this: "His heart is harder than a rock!" Here, hard-heartedness is tied to Leviathan. There is no compassion, grace, or mercy within his cold and hardened heart. Pride that has solidified into stubbornness is one of his characteristics and is used by the Dragon with much success.

Principality	Devices (Purposes)	Tactics (Methods)	Weapons
Dragon	Divide, destroy	"Twist and separate"	Pride, offense, jealousy, stubbornness

The primary tactics of the Dragon are to twist and separate. He seeks to twist the view and perceptions of a person by fostering pride, offense, and jealousy. The Dragon then uses stubbornness to put a wedge between people and cause them to separate.

In the following verse, the Dragon is pictured as dwelling in the middle of the Nile and is thus associated with Egypt and pride.

Ezekiel 29:3 NASB
*Speak and say, 'Thus says the Lord God, "Behold, I am against you, Pharaoh, king of Egypt, The great monster [**tanniyn**] that lies in the midst of his rivers, That has said, 'My Nile is mine, and I myself have made it.'*

In the end times, the Dragon will be primarily responsible for setting up the kingdom of the Antichrist and for giving power to the beast and the false prophet. This will be his time for great boasting and it will seem that his pride has been justified in ruling the world. However, it is only for a short time!

Revelation 13:4-5 KJV
And they worshipped the dragon which gave power unto the beast: and they worshipped the beast, saying, Who is like unto the beast? who is able to make war with him?
And there was given unto him a mouth speaking great things and blasphemies; and power was given unto him to continue forty and two months.

PRACTICAL APPLICATION

The firm platform of the gospel of peace enables us to stand against the principality of the Dragon. Belief in the truth that every person has a particular place and function in the body of Christ effectively nullifies divisions and competition between people.

Pride is often the root cause of divisions because it is associated with strife. The opposite of a prideful mindset is to be humble, willing to listen and receive counsel and advice.

Proverbs 13:10 NIV
Where there is strife, there is pride, but wisdom is found in those who take advice.

The opposite of pride is humility, which is the first step in keeping the unity of the Spirit in the bond of peace.

Ephesians 4:1-4 ESV
I therefore, a prisoner for the Lord, urge you to walk in a manner worthy of the calling to which you have been called,
with all humility and gentleness, with patience, bearing with one another in love,

eager to maintain the unity of the Spirit in the bond of peace.
There is one body and one Spirit – just as you were called to the one
hope that belongs to your call.

The verbal action behind the word humility in Aramaic, **mak,** is to lie down flat or lie down under. This indicates submission to one another (1 Peter 5:5). We need to be willing to listen to each other, truly listen, in order to appreciate our differences as well as to confirm the oneness we have in the Spirit. Humility is crucial to maintaining unity. Then we need to put on gentleness, longsuffering and forbearance in order to negate the weapon of pride. This is a lifetime pursuit.

We each have a special place, a special function, and no one person is any less or more important than anyone else. That is the firm platform provided by God to give us a wonderful way to function and give in the one body of Christ. The sandals of the gospel of peace are especially important for ministers and leaders. Those in a position of leadership are sometimes tricked by the Enemy into manipulating people to follow them. Leaders have a natural ability to motivate others to follow them, and this ability can be misdirected. When we truly believe that each person is important, we do not need to force unity through manipulation or intimidation. Leaders should encourage each person in the body to function with Christ as the head.

Another weapon of the Dragon is offense. When someone has been offended, the practical application of the sandals allows for multiple times of forgiveness. Peter asked Jesus how many times he should forgive his brother and Peter said he could probably muster seven times. Then Jesus said, "I do not say to you seven times, but seventy-seven times" (Matthew 18:21-22). In other words, MANY times!

Offense is the "bait of Satan" as described by John Bevere. It pulls one into the captivity of wrath and bitterness and hatred, as the bait of a snare draws an animal into the trap.[31] When we forgive those who hurt us, no matter who is right or wrong, we imitate our heavenly

---

[31] John Bevere, *The Bait of Satan*, pp. 6-7.

Father's kindness and mercy. Jesus told a parable about a king who forgave his servant a very large debt (Matthew 18:23-34), the amount of the offense being roughly equivalent to $6,000,000,000 in current U.S. currency. The servant then demanded return of a debt from his fellow servant – about $10,000 by current standards – a mere fraction of the huge debt he had been forgiven. When we harbor offenses, we have not realized what God has forgiven us for.

Another temptation orchestrated by the Dragon brings up the question of who is the greatest or who should have the most recognition. When James and John asked who would sit at the right or left hand of Jesus Christ (in other words, who would be the greatest), Jesus said that the greatest leader needed to be the greatest servant.

Mark 10:42-45 KJV
But Jesus called them to him, and saith unto them, Ye know that they which are accounted to rule over the Gentiles exercise lordship over them; and their great ones exercise authority upon them.
But so shall it not be among you: but whosoever will be great among you, shall be your minister:
And whosoever of you will be the chiefest, shall be servant of all.
For even the Son of man came not to be ministered unto, but to minister, and to give his life a ransom for many.

Sometime later, the disciples were still arguing over who would be greatest in the kingdom of heaven. The Lord, who was the greatest leader, taught them a valuable lesson in a memorable way. Jesus washed the disciple's feet and showed them this critical principle of leadership by example.

John 13:12-17 APNT
And after he had washed their feet, he took up his garments and sat and said to them, "Do you know what I have done to you?
You call me 'our Master and our Lord' and you speak well, for I am.
If therefore I, your Lord and your Master, have washed your feet for you, how much more ought you to wash the feet of one another?
For I have given you this example, that you should also do as I have done for you.

Truly, truly I say to you, there is no servant who is greater than his lord and there is no apostle who is greater than him who sent him. If you understand these [things], you are blessed if you will do them.

What is amazing is that after the day of Pentecost there are no further records of this argument about who was the greatest of the apostles!

We stand together in unity in the body of Christ because we each have the same gift of the measure of Christ. When we allow the peace of Christ to rule in our hearts, we will negate the tactics of the Dragon who wants to cause division.

Colossians 3:15 APNT
And the peace of Christ will govern your hearts, for to him you were called in one body. And be thankful to Christ.

When we believe that each person has his own place in the body of Christ, there is no room for offense and jealousy to gain a foothold. We can each be thankful for all we have been given in Christ and stand against any separations caused by the Dragon. We can refuse to be divided by continuing to forgive others in the body of Christ, and by encouraging each person's individual function with Christ as the true leader.

Chapter 9
THE SHIELD OF THE NAME OF JESUS CHRIST

ACTION WE TAKE	PIECE OF ARMOR	SPIRITUAL CLOTHING	AGAINST PRINCIPALITY
Raise up	shield	of the name of Jesus Christ	Satan

The word "shield" in Ephesians 6:16 is the Greek word **thureos** and comes from the word for door. The Roman shield was large and oblong, shaped like a door, four feet by two and a half feet, and sometimes curved on the inner side. The inner core was made of wood, with up to six layers of leather covering it. The leather in these layers was tightly woven together and tanned so that they became almost as strong as steel. The center of the shield often had a metal knob, called a boss, which could be used offensively.

The first characteristic we should note about the shield is that it covered the soldier's entire body. Its second unique quality is that it was designed to be clipped or stacked tightly together to form various formations in the line of a battle. The soldier carried the sizable shield on his left arm and held his sword by the handle, with the blade down, in his right hand. One Roman battle formation using the shield was called the **testudo**, or tortoise. A cohort of soldiers (approximately 80 men) would stand together, those in the front line carried their shields in front of them and those in subsequent lines carried them over their heads, to effectively make a box. Protected on all sides, they would use this formation to invade enemy lines, advancing little by little.

We will soon see how this battle strategy applies spiritually to the believer's use of the shield.

Ephesians 6:16 KJV
Above all, taking the shield of faith, wherewith ye shall be able to quench all the fiery darts of the wicked.

"Above all" does not mean that this is the most important piece of armor. The Greek translation is somewhat ambiguous; the Aramaic says more definitely, "and with these," meaning that the first three pieces of the armor (the belt, breastplate and sandals) are now to be associated with the next three pieces (the shield, helmet and sword). Several authors describing the armor have noted that the last three pieces of the armor are to be taken into battle, whereas the first three need to be worn at all times.[32] The most important word in the beginning portion of this verse is "taking."

"Take" is the Greek word **analambano,** which can be translated, "take up," or "raise up." The soldier put the shield into action by raising it up either in front of his body or over his head. If the shield was lying on the ground, it provided no protection. The same may be said of the believer's shield. It provides no benefit unless it is utilized.

Now what is this shield of faith? It is crucial for us to know what the shield is and how it works spiritually.

Faith in this verse is not what we do; it is what we have in Christ, so in Ephesians 6:16, the use of "faith" has to be a figure of speech, where "faith" takes the place of what we have faith in. This figure is called *metonymy* (of the effect).[33] With very few exceptions, faith or trust is always in someone or something − it has an object. Lloyd-Jones explains this succinctly:

---

[32] D. Martyn Lloyd-Jones, *A Christian Soldier*, pp. 296-297.
[33] E.W. Bullinger, *Figures of Speech Used in the Bible*, p. 565.

But how does faith act as our shield? The answer is that faith never points to itself, it always points to its object. That is absolutely crucial…if you put your faith in faith you are eventually undone….Faith never protects a man in and of itself.[34]

The object of faith is God and what he has provided in Christ. God is often called a shield in the Old Testament. David relied on God for his protection and covering. His trust was in God, not himself.

Psalm 144:1-2 ESV
Blessed be the LORD, my rock, who trains my hands for war, and my fingers for battle;
he is my steadfast love and my fortress, my stronghold and my deliverer, my shield and he in whom I take refuge, who subdues peoples under me.

Romans 1:5 identifies the object of faith in relation to the armor.

Romans 1:5 APNT
By whom we have received grace and apostleship among all the Gentiles, so that they would obey the faith of his name,

Here "faith" represents the authority of the name of Jesus Christ. The faith of his name is the power to use the name of Jesus Christ. In Matthew 28:18, Jesus commissioned the disciples by saying, "All authority in heaven and on earth has been given to me. Therefore go…" (NIV). Ephesians 1:20-23 makes it clear that all things are under the feet of Christ and he is the head over all things to the church. His name is greater than "every name that is named."

Philippians 2:9-10 KJV
Wherefore God also hath highly exalted him, and given him a name which is above every name:
That at the name of Jesus every knee should bow, of things in heaven, and things in earth, and things under the earth;

---

[34] D. Martyn Lloyd-Jones, *A Christian Soldier*, p. 305.

The Aramaic word picture for the name Jesus is "the power of change completely experienced." Change is accomplished because of Jesus being the deliverer. Chris Tomlin has written a song about the name of Jesus that summarizes the freedom available with the faith of his name.

> The name of Jesus is a refuge
> A shelter from the storm, a help to those who call
> The name of Jesus is a fortress
> A saving place to run, a hope unshakable
> When we fall You are the Savior, when we call You are the answer
> There is power in Your name, there is power in Your name
> In the name of Jesus
> There is life and healing
> Chains are broken in Your name
> Every knee will bow down and our hearts will cry out
> Songs of freedom in Your name, oh, in Your name

We can understand the power of being able to use his name in the context of being an ambassador from one country to another. The ambassador is not important in and of himself, but when he speaks for his country, he has the authority of his country to back up what he says. He is the one who actually speaks the words, but the power behind his words is that of his country.

As a faithful ambassador speaks on behalf of his country, we have the privilege and responsibility in any situation to use the greatest name of all to exercise the power and authority we have been given. Peter and John used his name in this way when they healed the lame man at the Beautiful Gate of the temple. Peter said, "Silver and gold have I none, but such as I have give I thee. In the name of Jesus Christ of Nazareth rise up and walk" (Acts 3:6). Peter said "such as I have..." He knew that he had the right to use the name of Jesus. It was Peter who actually spoke and acted, but he was enabled to heal the man in the inherent power of the name of Jesus Christ.

Acts 3 describes an exchange between Peter and the religious leaders when Peter was confronted for healing the lame man. He boldly proclaimed that he had healed the lame man by the "faith of his name." The NET Bible clarifies the account even more.

Acts 3:16 NET
And on the basis of faith in Jesus' name, his very name has made this man – whom you see and know – strong. The faith that is through Jesus has given him this complete health in the presence of you all.

Acts 3:16 APNT
And by the faith of his name he has strengthened and healed this [man], whom you see and know, and faith that is in him [Christ] has given him [the man] this wholeness before all of you.

We raise up the shield which is the power of the name of Jesus Christ, to command deliverance from ALL the fiery darts of the Evil One. The principality that this piece of armor goes against is Satan. We can understand some of his tactics when we look at the characteristics of the fiery darts that he launches. In Roman battles, darts were long pieces of cane shaped into arrows filled with combustible fluids that exploded on impact. The purpose of the fiery arrow was to alarm the soldier, making him afraid of what was happening to his shield so that he would throw it down and try to run away from the fire.

When a soldier prepared for battle, he would coat his shield with oil so the leather would not get stiff and brittle. This would prevent the shield from becoming ineffective or actually breaking during the heat of battle. The soldier would also soak the shield in water before the battle. This would enable the shield to snuff out and ultimately quench the fiery darts before they exploded. In one description of a battle, a soldier had 200 arrows stuck in his shield at the end of the siege, but not one of them had burst into flames!

Many believers are being hit by the Enemy's fiery arrows every day because they are not raising their shields and using the name of Jesus Christ. They also have not anointed the shield with the "oil" of the Spirit or saturated it with the "water" of the Word. One target Satan aims at is our emotions. The flaming arrows are designed not only to hit us, but also to enflame us, like a fire that is burning out of control. For example, we get hit with some kind of sickness and it bursts into flames of fear, worry, anger and rage.

Jesus Christ is the name to which every knee must bow (Philippians 2:10). The shield of faith is the authority to use the name of Jesus Christ against the fiery arrows which will inevitably come our way. The "faith of his name" will absolutely quench ALL these attacks.

PRINCIPALITY OF SATAN

"Satan" is a transliteration of the Hebrew word **satan** for "opponent" or "adversary". Satan is the principality that sends fiery darts to oppose and overcome people. Every action he takes is opposed to the purposes of God. The first use of "satan" in the Bible is in the record of Balaam. An angel of the Lord opposed Balaam while he was on the road in direct disobedience to God's instruction, as he accompanied the princes of Moab. This verse shows the simple meaning of "adversary."

Numbers 22:22 KJV
*And God's anger was kindled because he went: and the angel of the LORD stood in the way for an adversary [**satan**] against him. Now he was riding upon his ass, and his two servants were with him.*

A "satan" is "one who withstands or stands against someone else." Some teachers have compared Satan to a prosecuting attorney in a court of law, but according to eastern custom there was no one person who had that role in legal cases. In the East, there was usually a witness who brought the charges against the accused. In Job, the "satan" is the accusing witness who is opposing Job.[35]

---

[35] *Dictionary of Deities and Demons in the Bible*, p. 728.

Job 1:6-9 KJV
Now there was a day when the sons of God came to present themselves before the LORD, and Satan came also among them.
And the LORD said unto Satan, Whence comest thou? Then Satan answered the LORD, and said, From going to and fro in the earth, and from walking up and down in it.
And the LORD said unto Satan, Hast thou considered my servant Job, that there is none like him in the earth, a perfect and an upright man, one that feareth God, and escheweth evil?
Then Satan answered the LORD, and said, Doth Job fear God for nought?

Satan continues to present himself as the witness and claims that if Job lost his prosperity and even his health, he would not continue to worship God. He then uses this opportunity to cause Job's torment. The purposes of Satan are to torment and oppress. He uses the weapons of fear, sickness, and catastrophes to shock a person and freeze him in his tracks, rendering him unable to see any way out.

Principality	Devices (Purposes)	Tactics (Methods)	Weapons
Satan	Torment, oppress	"Shock and freeze"	Fear, sickness, catastrophes

Fear always causes torment.

1 John 4:18 KJV
There is no fear in love; but perfect love casteth out fear: because fear hath torment. He that feareth is not made perfect in love.

While the main weapon of the Dragon is pride, the main weapon of Satan is fear. There are so many different kinds of fears! And they all include torment that imposes a form of punishment on the person experiencing the fear. Perry Stone describes it like this: "All fear plants seeds of the idea of something bad happening, or of a penalty or retaliation."[36]

There are many manifestations of fear caused by Satan. Earthquakes, hurricanes, fire and terminal illness are just a few of the many scenarios that cause fear. Fear causes terror. As a result, distress occurs because the fearful one is unable to envision a remedy. In this passage of Proverbs, God describes the effects of fear as a desolation or storm.

Proverbs 1:26-27 KJV
I also will laugh at your calamity; I will mock when your fear cometh; When your fear cometh as desolation, and your destruction cometh as a whirlwind; when distress and anguish cometh upon you.

Another purpose of Satan is to oppress. Someone can be oppressed by Satan when they are incited to behave contrary to God's will. This was the case in 1 Chronicles 21:1 when "Satan stood up against Israel, and provoked David to number Israel." David numbered Israel even though he knew God did not want him to do it, and even after Joab advised him not to. Taking a census was contrary to God's will because according to Exodus 30:12, a man only had the right to count or number what belonged to him. Israel didn't belong to David; Israel belonged to God. It was up to God to command a counting of Israel, as he did in Exodus, but only after receiving ransom money to "atone" for the counting. Although David recognized his error, there were grave consequences and 70,000 men died because of his sin.

Any enticement that lures someone to oppose God is a tactic of Satan and needs to be exposed by revelation from God. In Acts 5, Satan filled Ananias' heart to keep back part of the price of the land that he had sold. He had the freedom to give whatever amount he wanted, but he lied regarding the price of the land. God showed Peter exactly what had happened and exposed the lies.

---

[36] Perry Stone, *There's a Crack in Your Armor*, p. 43.

THE SHIELD OF THE NAME OF JESUS CHRIST

Acts 5:3 APNT
And Simon said to him, Ananias, why is it that Satan has so filled your
heart that you should lie to the Holy Spirit and hide some of the money
of the sale of the field?

The consequences were severe to Ananias and Sapphira. They died
because of the actions they took.

The shield of the name of Jesus Christ will protect the believer against
any kind of fear, and walking by the Spirit will expose whether or not
a proposed action or situation is opposed to God's will.

PRACTICAL APPLICATION

When Paul was on a ship on his way to Rome, the ship was caught in
a treacherous storm. Days went by without any hope of rescue. Can
you imagine the fear of the whole crew? But Paul was steadfast in
prayer for fourteen days until he received this answer.

Acts 27:20-25 KJV
And when neither sun nor stars in many days appeared, and no small
tempest lay on us, all hope that we should be saved was then taken
away.
But after long abstinence Paul stood forth in the midst of them, and
said, Sirs, ye should have hearkened unto me, and not have loosed
from Crete, and to have gained this harm and loss.
And now I exhort you to be of good cheer: for there shall be no loss
of any man's life among you, but of the ship.
For there stood by me this night the angel of God, whose I am, and
whom I serve,
Saying, Fear not, Paul; thou must be brought before Caesar: and, lo,
God hath given thee all them that sail with thee.
Wherefore, sirs, be of good cheer: for I believe God, that it shall be
even as it was told me.

Paul refused to be frozen in fear by the storm, and continued in prayer until he got an answer from God. As a result, all the people on the ship were successfully saved.

A catastrophe can be a physical storm or something unexpected. There was a recent tragedy in Las Vegas, where a man opened fire on a crowd of concert-goers, wounding and killing many people. The shock must have been very great since it was so unexpected. I heard about several policemen at the concert who immediately went into action once the shooting started. They had been trained to quickly overcome the shock of a situation and promptly engage to help people. However, many people in the crowd were frozen and immobilized by the fear that immediately set in. This is the type of situation where as believers, we need to immediately negate the effect of fear and begin using the name of Jesus Christ. I am certain there were Christians in that location who contributed greatly to helping people.

I recently had an example of overcoming fear in my own life when my hands broke out in a red, itchy rash. I had never had anything like this before and tried a number of topical ointments, but they did not help and the rash was getting worse. I found out that it was a kind of eczema via searching medical websites and tried things that normally work for that. Still no better! Now I was becoming fearful – it is amazing how many things we use our hands for each day. But I did not give up! After spending much time in prayer, I received an answer that led me to a particular natural product that I did not know anything about. When I got some and applied it, it worked and my recovery was quick. When we are in a situation that does not get resolved right away, we need to persist in prayer (like Paul in the storm) to find the answer! We need to seek revelation from God about what to do.

Another example of Satan using a catastrophe to cause great fear is a forecast of disaster threatening to destroy people and their property. Recently hurricanes landed on the southern United States and started a path inland. There was so much news coverage of these events that many Christians were praying. Both storms were destructive, but not

nearly as devastating as the fear-instilling news had predicted. That
is what happens when many Christians put their shields together (like
the Roman tortoise formation) and use the name of Jesus Christ to
thwart an attack.

We need to stand with each other to help defeat the Enemy, especially
when someone gets weary of the battle. In the Old Testament, even
the great warrior David needed help. Though David had defeated the
giant Goliath in his youth and the Philistines afterwards, later in his
life, four giants (who were descendants of Goliath) came to try to kill
him.

2 Samuel 21:15-22 ESV
*There was war again between the Philistines and Israel, and David
went down together with his servants, and they fought against the
Philistines. And David grew weary.*
*And Ishbi-benob, one of the descendants of the giants, whose spear
weighed three hundred shekels of bronze, and who was armed with a
new sword, thought to kill David.*
*But Abishai the son of Zeruiah came to his aid and attacked the
Philistine and killed him. Then David's men swore to him, "You shall
no longer go out with us to battle, lest you quench the lamp of Israel."*
*After this there was again war with the Philistines at Gob. Then
Sibbecai the Hushathite struck down Saph, who was one of the
descendants of the giants.*
*And there was again war with the Philistines at Gob, and Elhanan
the son of Jaare-oregim, the Bethlehemite, struck down Goliath the
Gittite, the shaft of whose spear was like a weaver's beam.*
*And there was again war at Gath, where there was a man of great
stature, who had six fingers on each hand, and six toes on each foot,
twenty-four in number, and he also was descended from the giants.*
*And when he taunted Israel, Jonathan the son of Shimei, David's
brother, struck him down.*
*These four were descended from the giants in Gath, and they fell by
the hand of David and by the hand of his servants.*

There is great power available when an individual uses the name of Jesus Christ, but when we are standing together we will see even greater results. Raise up the shield of the name and authority of Jesus Christ and persist using it until there is victory! Stand together with shields locked together and help to take down any giants who try to attack. Walk by the Spirit to see where the opposition is coming from and then determine by God's revelation how to best stand against it.

Chapter 10
THE HELMET OF REDEMPTION

ACTION WE TAKE	PIECE OF ARMOR	SPIRITUAL CLOTHING	AGAINST PRINCIPALITY
Set on your head	helmet	of redemption	Belial

We are to set on our head the helmet of redemption. The word "helmet" in Aramaic is **sanirtha** and could be translated "turban." When I was in Israel, I saw many people, whether Arabs or Jews, wearing scarves that were wound around the head into turbans. The different colors identified them to others. The same was true regarding the Roman helmets. They had various plumes and decorations which identified the rank of the soldier, such as a centurion, tribune, etc. Redemption is what identifies a believer.

"Redemption," which is the Aramaic word used in Ephesians 6:17, is more accurate here than "salvation." Redemption includes salvation, but it is much deeper.

There are three key parts to redemption:

1. We are bought with a price
2. We are delivered from the power of darkness
3. We are redeemed to a life of freedom

91

THE HELMET OF REDEMPTION

1 Peter 1:18-19 KJV
Forasmuch as ye know that ye were not redeemed with corruptible things, as silver and gold, from your vain conversation received by tradition from your fathers;
But with the precious blood of Christ, as of a lamb without blemish and without spot:

A price was paid for our redemption and that price was the precious blood of Christ. As the Passover lamb, his blood was poured out on the mercy seat as an atonement for sin, once and for all. There is no need of any more sacrifices for sin; it is completely paid for. In this way, redemption is like justification. We could not and cannot earn our redemption. As the lyrics in the song *In Christ Alone* so aptly state:

> There in the ground His body lay
> Light of the world by darkness slain
> Then bursting forth in glorious Day
> Up from the grave He rose again
> And as He stands in victory
> Sin's curse has lost its grip on me
> For I am His and He is mine
> Bought with the precious blood of Christ.

We stand in victory because of his victory!

Colossians 1:12-13 APNT
You should give thanks to God the Father, who has made us worthy for a portion of the inheritance of the holy [ones] in light
and has delivered us from the authority of darkness and has transferred us to the kingdom of his beloved Son.

We have been rescued, delivered, and redeemed from the authority of darkness. Imagine that we are on a train speeding down the track to a point where it goes straight off a cliff. Just before this happens, we are "snatched' out of the train and rescued from the sure death and destruction that awaits us. In the same way, we have been delivered from a great death by the sacrifice of Jesus Christ.

THE HELMET OF REDEMPTION

2 Corinthians 1:10 KJV
Who delivered us from so great a death, and doth deliver: in whom
we trust that he will yet deliver us;

In English, when we say "we have been delivered" we are referring
to something that has been accomplished in the past. But in the
Eastern way of thinking, deliverance is past, present and future. God
has delivered us (we received his Spirit) and **does deliver** (now,
present tense) and he will **yet deliver us** (in the future). Our
redemption will be complete when we receive our new bodies and are
forever with the Lord. The helmet of redemption is instrumental in
our present tense deliverance now.

Go back and look at the end of Colossians 1:13: "he has transferred
us to the kingdom of his beloved Son." It is not enough to know that
we were rescued in the past. We need to be rescued continually and
redeemed every day! But what have we been redeemed for? We are
not just hanging in mid-air with no place to go. We have been
transferred to Christ's kingdom. Redemption is always from one
thing TO something else.

We are redeemed from death TO life.
We are redeemed from slavery TO freedom.
We are redeemed from darkness TO light.
We are redeemed from being strangers and foreigners TO being sons
with an inheritance.

Galatians 4:4-7 KJV
But when the fulness of the time was come, God sent forth his Son,
made of a woman, made under the law,
To redeem them that were under the law, that we might receive the
adoption of sons.
And because ye are sons, God hath sent forth the Spirit of his Son into
your hearts, crying, Abba, Father.
Wherefore thou art no more a servant, but a son; and if a son, then
an heir of God through Christ.

Hallelujah! We need to be living in redemption right now. The helmet is called the "hope of salvation" in 1 Thessalonians 5:8. Hope is also not just future. Yes, there is an ultimate redemption, but we are to be living in the freedom and light of redemption every single day. The Aramaic word for "to hope" is **sevar** and its simplest meaning is "to think." What are we thinking about? The hope of redemption gives us the courage to continue to live as sons and heirs of God through Christ.

PRINCIPALITY OF BELIAL

The helmet of redemption helps us stand against the principality of Belial who tries to get us to "stay on the train." Belial is a compound word in Hebrew meaning "without worth or profit." He causes a sense of unworthiness in people by tempting them to be involved in perverse and detrimental activities. The Hebrew verb from which Belial is derived is **bali** which means "to wear out" (such as a garment). Other scholars have derived the name Belial from **bli**, to swallow, hence the name, "swallower." [37] That is a very apt picture because the wickedness of this principality is designed to swallow people up with bondage of every kind. "Devour" in Aramaic is **bela**, and means to swallow or completely overpower.

2 Corinthians 2:7 APNT
And from now on the contrary, you ought to forgive him and to comfort him, so that he who is such should not be swallowed up [**bela**] *in excessive sorrow.*

The term is used 27 times in the King James Version and usually occurs in such expressions as "son(s) of Belial" or "daughter of Belial." This is what the sons of Eli were called.

1 Samuel 2:12 KJV
Now the sons of Eli were sons of Belial; they knew not the LORD.

---

[37] *Theological Wordbook of the Old Testament*, p. 111.

Other translations call the sons of Eli "worthless men." They lay with the women who were serving at the entrance to the tent of meeting (1 Samuel 2:22). They disregarded the proper use of the animals brought for sacrifice and used force to make the servants give them the meat that belonged in the sacrifice.

1 Samuel 2:13-17 ESV
The custom of the priests with the people was that when any man offered sacrifice, the priest's servant would come, while the meat was boiling, with a three-pronged fork in his hand,
and he would thrust it into the pan or kettle or cauldron or pot. All that the fork brought up the priest would take for himself. This is what they did at Shiloh to all the Israelites who came there.
Moreover, before the fat was burned, the priest's servant would come and say to the man who was sacrificing, "Give meat for the priest to roast, for he will not accept boiled meat from you but only raw."
And if the man said to him, "Let them burn the fat first, and then take as much as you wish," he would say, "No, you must give it now, and if not, I will take it by force."
Thus the sin of the young men was very great in the sight of the LORD, for the men treated the offering of the LORD with contempt.

A number of words are used to describe a man of Belial. In Proverbs 6:12 (NET), the "naughty" man is equated with the wicked man, or one who is lawless. He "walks around saying perverse things." "A worthless man plots evil, and his speech is like a scorching fire" (Proverbs 16:27 ESV). He is called a "wicked counselor" (Nahum 1:11 NASB). "A corrupt [**beliya`al**] witness makes a mockery of justice; the mouth of the wicked gulps down evil" (Proverbs 19:28 NLT).

Nabal, Abigail's husband, is also called a man of Belial. "Folly" is the Hebrew word **nebalah**, which means foolishness, but also "immorality with profane actions." When David and his men had performed a service of protection during sheep shearing time, Nabal contemptuously refused to pay them anything. He is described as "surly and mean." Later, his own men comment, "He's so ill-tempered that no one can even talk to him!" (1 Samuel 25:17 NLT)

THE HELMET OF REDEMPTION

1 Samuel 25:25 KJV
Let not my lord, I pray thee, regard this man of Belial, even Nabal:
for as his name is, so is he; Nabal is his name, and folly is with him:
but I thine handmaid saw not the young men of my lord, whom thou
didst send.

The tactics of this principality are to "corrupt and distress." Belial
gets people involved in folly of every kind, causing them to corrupt
their morals. His weapons are unworthiness and any kind of
perversity, whether in the category of sexual lusts, addictions, or
corruption of the tongue and habits.

Principality	Devices (Purposes)	Tactics, Schemes	Weapons
Belial	Captivate, Swallow	"Corrupt and distress"	Unworthiness, addictions, perversity

King Ahab had desired a vineyard that was close to the palace which
belonged to a man named Naboth. Jezebel used men of Belial to give
false testimony regarding Naboth's vineyard to get it for him, in spite
of taking his family inheritance in the process.

1 Kings 21:13 KJV
And there came in two men, children of Belial, and sat before him:
and the men of Belial witnessed against him, even against Naboth, in
the presence of the people, saying, Naboth did blaspheme God and
the king. Then they carried him forth out of the city, and stoned him
with stones, that he died.

The second part of Belial's tactics is to cause extreme distress (and
even death) because of corruption. This could be by someone else, as
in this case, or it could be the result of personal addiction or
perversity.

The part of the armor for dealing with the principality of Belial is the helmet of redemption because all people involved in this kind of corruption need to be redeemed from slavery to freedom.

PRACTICAL APPLICATION

Distress is often the result of the actions of other people who are corrupt. For example, a person may experience distress when he loses his job after 30 years because of a corrupt boss or co-worker. But if this disappointment is allowed to fester in the mind and grow larger and larger, depression sets in. Depression is a good example of "swallowing" because it eventually immobilizes the person. Stress is a rampant problem in our culture and most people resort to some kind of panacea, such as alcohol or TV or any number of things, to try to alleviate the resulting distress. The truth is that none of those things bring deliverance – only the helmet of redemption!

Titus 2:14 APNT
Who gave himself for us, so that he could deliver us from all wickedness and would purify for himself a new people who are zealous in good works.

In these types of situations, we need "snatching" off the train and the deliverance happens when we give everything up to God. A few years ago we had an Amazon bookstore and we got charged a huge long-term storage fee because we had bought the business from a man who was not honest about the inventory. We spent several months pursuing all kinds of things to solve the problem. I was stressed because Amazon had frozen all our sales. It didn't seem that there was any solution. One day, I just threw up my hands and said, "I give this all to you, God!" That day the credit came through. There were more challenges with the bookstore, but I learned a great lesson that day – that I had to let God fight our battles and REDEEM us.

Many times, we need what I call "mini-hopes." Hope is an expectation that something good will happen. If we lose our job, the expectation is that there will be another job in the future. That is a mini-hope. It is the confidence that we will be delivered from the derailing train on a daily basis and be brought into a place of freedom and life. Sometimes, the deliverance might not be immediate, but the confidence is there that it <u>will</u> happen. David found hope in his struggles with various enemies.

Psalm 16:8-9 KJV
I have set the LORD always before me: because he is at my right hand, I shall not be moved.
Therefore my heart is glad, and my glory rejoiceth: my flesh also shall rest in hope.

David set the Lord and what he said always before him – not the problem, or the wicked ones causing the problem, or the way he was feeling at the time. Remember the turban that was mentioned in the beginning of the chapter? Here that turban is the hope of being able to overcome even death. It was wrapped tightly around David's mind. Everywhere he looked, he saw only the Lord. THEREFORE he was not moved or shaken or stressed!

Joy is also a great key to walking and living in redemption. Rejoicing because the solution is coming will prevent us from being worn down and swallowed up with distress because of people or situations around us. Do you remember how the helmet identifies us? When people see us rejoicing in the middle of trying experiences, they can identify us as REDEEMED believers!

Psalm 118:5 ESV
Out of my distress I called on the LORD; the LORD answered me and set me free.

David dealt with sons of Belial in his own camp. When his band was away from their home in Ziklag, the Amalekites came and raided the city and took all the wives and children captive.

1 Samuel 30:1-6 ESV
Now when David and his men came to Ziklag on the third day, the
Amalekites had made a raid against the Negeb and against Ziklag.
They had overcome Ziklag and burned it with fire
and taken captive the women and all who were in it, both small and
great. They killed no one, but carried them off and went their way.
And when David and his men came to the city, they found it burned
with fire, and their wives and sons and daughters taken captive.
Then David and the people who were with him raised their voices and
wept until they had no more strength to weep.
David's two wives also had been taken captive, Ahinoam of Jezreel
and Abigail the widow of Nabal of Carmel.
And David was greatly distressed, for the people spoke of stoning
him, because all the people were bitter in soul, each for his sons and
daughters. But David strengthened himself in the LORD his God.

David was in great distress, not only because the people wanted to
stone him, but also because he did not know what had happened to
his wives and children. Can you imagine the thoughts going through
his mind about the worst possible circumstances? David did not give
in to the distress; he strengthened himself in God and went to him to
determine what to do about the situation. He recovered everything the
Amalekites had taken away. Two hundred men had not gone with
David to the battle, because they were faint. After they returned with
the spoil, men of Belial opposed sharing the victory with these men
who had stayed behind.

1 Samuel 30:22 KJV
Then answered all the wicked men and men of Belial, of those that
went with David, and said, Because they went not with us, we will not
give them ought of the spoil that we have recovered, save to every
man his wife and his children, that they may lead them away, and
depart.

David did not tolerate the influence of the sons of Belial and divided
the spoil equally.

No matter what the circumstances, we must also be strengthened in God and seek for his solution to every situation of distress. The hope of our redemption is confidence that there is deliverance available in every situation, even death.

1 Thessalonians 5:8 NLT
But let us who live in the light be clearheaded, protected by the armor of faith and love, and wearing as our helmet the confidence of our salvation.

The practical application of this piece of armor is useful especially in times of sudden loss, perhaps the death of a dear one or a family member. There is no comfort greater than knowing that death does not have the ultimate victory. A day will come when we will be able to say, "O death, where is they sting? O grave, where is thy victory?" (1 Corinthians 15:55) This Old Testament verse quoted here is from Hosea 13:14 and begins, "I will ransom them from the power of the grave."

Hebrews 6:19 says that our hope is like an anchor for a ship.

Hebrews 6:19 APNT
Which we have as an anchor that holds our soul, so that it is not shaken and it enters within the veil.

The word "shaken" is used of an earthquake. The wicked things that happen in life can certainly shake us like an earthquake, but the helmet of redemption brings protection for our mind and "holds our soul." Let's continue to live in redemption day by day until the Lord returns!

Chapter 11
THE SWORD OF THE SPIRIT, THE LIVING WORD

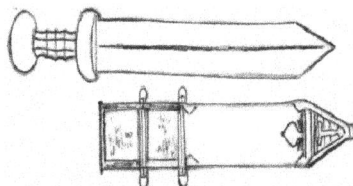

ACTION WE TAKE	PIECE OF ARMOR	SPIRITUAL CLOTHING	AGAINST PRINCIPALITY
Take hold of, clasp	sword	of the Spirit, the living Word	Serpent

The last piece of the armor is the sword that belongs to the Spirit. The sword is both an offensive and defensive weapon; thus it differs somewhat from the defensive pieces we have looked at so far.

The Greek word for "sword" is **machaira** and refers to a two-edged sword, approximately 19 inches long. The tip or point of the blade was extremely sharp. It was used in close combat, primarily as a thrusting or cutting weapon. Rick Renner notes in *Dressed to Kill* that "this two-edged blade inflicted a wound far worse than the other swords." Once a Roman soldier thrust the sword into the torso of his enemy, he would give it a wrenching twist so that the entrails would spill out as the soldier pulled the sword from the enemy's body.[38] In close combat, this weapon would be extremely effective against the enemy.

The Roman term for the sword used in the first century is **gladius.** The Roman sword was adapted from a Spanish design and was forged

---

[38] Rick Renner, *Dressed to Kill*, p. 406, 410.

out of iron, lightweight enough to be flexible and sturdy enough to pierce through even heavy metal armor. The blade was sharpened to a razor's edge. Much of the training of soldiers revolved around how to use this weapon. It was not the sweeping action of the sword that killed. The stabbing action was what mortally wounded an enemy.

Hebrews 4:12 APNT
For the word of God is living and completely effective and sharper than a two-edged sword and enters all the way to the separation of soul and of spirit, and of the joints and of the marrow and of the bones, and judges the reasonings and the thoughts of the heart.

The all-powerful sword of the Word of God is sharper than any Roman gladius. When wielded by a son of God, its function is to cut straight to the core of a matter and uncover the truth. It is even able to separate the soul and spirit of a man.

The word for "joint" in Aramaic can also be translated "membrane, or covering." When I was studying a book on the human body, I found a beautiful illustration of the inside of a bone. The inside of a bone has three parts: the marrow (where the blood vessels are), surrounded by the actual bone cells and the outside membrane. This membrane is very hard and is called the periosteum. It would be extremely difficult to slice between these three parts because they are fused together to form the bone, yet the Word of God can separate them. This is how sharp the Word of God is!

The word for "word" in Ephesians 6:17 is **rhema,** which often has to do with the spoken word. A rhema is a "specific word or message…at a specific time and for a special purpose."[39] The Aramaic word is **meltha** and the root verb means, literally, "to speak."

---

[39] Rick Renner, *Dressed to Kill*, p. 408.

THE SWORD OF THE SPIRIT, THE LIVING WORD

John 6:63 ESV
It is the Spirit who gives life; the flesh is no help at all. The words
[rhema] *that I have spoken to you are spirit and life.*

Besides being spoken, **rhema** is the Word of God in application and
it brings life. When Jesus stood up in the temple and addressed the
Jews gathered there during the Feast of Tabernacles, he spoke about
how the gift of the Spirit would be like a river of living water. The
Lord alludes to a river spoken of in Zechariah 14:8 that will flow out
from Jerusalem in the millennial kingdom and water the whole land
of Israel. As the literal river will flow out of the inner part of
Jerusalem, so life-giving spiritual words flow from the heart of a
believer.

John 7:37-39 APNT
And on the high day, which is the last [day] of the feast, Jesus was
standing and he cried out and said, "If anyone is thirsty, he should
come to me and drink.
Whoever believes in me, as the scriptures have said, rivers of living
water will flow from his inner part."
Now he said this about the Spirit that those who believed in him were
about to receive, for the Spirit was not yet given, because Jesus was
not yet glorified.

The **rhema** of God, spoken in a specific situation, becomes a living
Word for that moment. Jesus Christ was the Word made flesh in his
physical body here on earth (John 1:14); he became the living Word,
showing forth the glory of the Father. Today the gift of the Spirit in
operation becomes a living Word of truth which also glorifies God
the Father.

In what way is this **rhema** Word of God a sword? God's Word
Translation is very specific regarding the sword of the Spirit.

Ephesians 6:17 GWT
Also, take salvation as your helmet and the word of God as the sword
that the Spirit supplies.

The sword of the Spirit is the **rhema** Word of God made living by the Spirit and supplied by the Spirit. This word is the application of a verse or scripture, or could be by revelation or inspiration, but it is never contrary to the written Word of God.

The sword is "two-edged," literally "having a double mouth," and is translated this way in both Greek and Aramaic. The Word of God has two mouths: one is written and the other is spoken. God's written Word is **logos** in Greek. When we utilize the written Word of God, and apply it to a particular situation it becomes a living Word and brings life to those who confess it. I think the best way to distinguish **logos** from **rhema** is this: **logos** is the core premise of a subject, while **rhema** is the premise in application. They can both be spoken, but the **rhema** is the "living Word" for that specific situation. Since they are two edges of the same sword, the written word and the spoken word cannot be separated. Just as a Roman soldier had to learn how to use his sword to be effective in battle, we need to study and meditate on the scriptures so that when we are attacked, we will know how to wield the sword.

This piece of the armor is integrally related to the belt of truth. The belt is what holds the sword. In the same way, God's faithfulness to his Word is the scabbard in which the Word in application rests. When the sword is wielded with precision, it is sharp and distinguishes truth from lies. This is the piece of the armor that enables us to stand against the Serpent.

PRINCIPALITY OF THE SERPENT

The Serpent was in the Garden of Eden; his Hebrew name is **nachash**. He is cunning and very subtle in his approach, using lies and half-truths. The origin of **nachash** may be onomatopoeic, derived from the hissing sound of a snake. This serpent is like a cobra or poisonous viper. The bite is venomous and the poison begins to permeate the victim's body immediately. The king cobra can grow up to 15 feet in length. It is known to eat other kinds of snakes. When the cobra is harassed, its body stands up and it makes a great hissing sound. This is the same description as the **nachash**. The denominative verb from **nachash** means "to practice divination." That means to conjure up something (like a dream or vision) that is not really there. An example is the vision of the witch of Endor conjuring up Samuel for King Saul. The name "Serpent" could also be rendered "the Deceiver."

In the Garden of Eden, the Serpent made the tree of the knowledge of good and evil appear as something that was desirable to eat. He used this deception to entice Eve to disobey God.

Genesis 3:1-6 KJV
Now the serpent [**nachash**] *was more subtil* [crafty] *than any beast of the field which the LORD God had made. And he said unto the woman, Yea, hath God said, Ye shall not eat of every tree of the garden?*
And the woman said unto the serpent, We may eat of the fruit of the trees of the garden:
But of the fruit of the tree which is in the midst of the garden, God hath said, Ye shall not eat of it, neither shall ye touch it, lest ye die.
And the serpent said unto the woman, Ye shall not surely die:
For God doth know that in the day ye eat thereof, then your eyes shall be opened, and ye shall be as gods, knowing good and evil.
And when the woman saw that the tree was good for food, and that it was pleasant to the eyes, and a tree to be desired to make one wise, she took of the fruit thereof, and did eat, and gave also unto her husband with her; and he did eat.

When the Serpent questioned Eve about what God had said, Eve left out the word "freely." She then spun her own interpretation of the Word of God by adding and changing it to "neither shall ye touch it, lest ye die." This erroneous statement informed the Serpent, who knew exactly what God had said, that Eve was not armed with the true Word of God and was therefore ready to be deceived.

The Serpent used three areas to deceive Eve: the lust of the flesh, the lust of the eyes and the pride of life (1 John 2:16). He first beguiled Eve to look at the tree and to notice that it was good for food (lust of the flesh). Then he stirred her to consider that it was pleasant to the eyes (lust of the eyes). Finally he deceived her into believing that the forbidden fruit was to be desired to make one wise (pride of life).

The Serpent always holds out enticing promises, most of which are either not true or impossible ("ye shall be as gods"). In dealing with Eve, he also questioned God's motives and implied that God was selfish and unfair in withholding that particular tree. When he finally had Eve hooked, he flatly contradicted what God had said by stating, "Ye shall not surely die." Eve ate the fruit and gave it to Adam, and their disobedience caused disastrous consequences for humanity – guilt, shame and death.[40]

The Evil One tried to use the same three temptations on Jesus. The first temptation was to turn stones into bread, which corresponds to the lust of the flesh. We discussed this in the chapter about *The Breastplate of Justification*. In Matthew 4 the second temptation of Jesus was the lust of the eyes, to see if God would save him no matter what he did. Again, the Serpent used what God had said which was true, but twisted it to try to deceive Jesus. The primary principality mentioned in the records of the temptations is the Devil, but I believe that all the principalities were at work together to try to defeat Jesus before he could even start his ministry.

Matthew 4:5-7 NET
Then the devil took him to the holy city, had him stand on the highest point of the temple,
and said to him, "If you are the Son of God, throw yourself down. For it is written, 'He will command his angels concerning you' and 'with their hands they will lift you up, so that you will not strike your foot against a stone.'"
Jesus said to him, "Once again it is written: 'You are not to put the Lord your God to the test.'"

The Lord is quoting Deuteronomy 6:16, "You shall not put the Lord your God to the test, as you tested him at Massah." Jesus did not deny

---

[40] Sydney Page, *Powers of Evil*, pp. 17-18.

that the Evil One had quoted the truth about angels, but casting himself down from the temple to prove that God would protect him would have been a wrong application of that verse. How did the children of Israel tempt God in Massah? They said, "Is the Lord among us or not?" (Exodus 17:1-7). After Israel had such proofs of his care and his kindness in rescuing them from the bondage of Egypt, God was provoked by their doubts that he would continue to do so every day. This quote from the Old Testament is a great example of how subtle the deceit of the Serpent can be. Jesus answered each temptation with "it is written" and correctly applied the scriptures to each situation.

The Evil One's third temptation of Jesus was to rule all the kingdoms of the earth and to be like God, which is the pride of life.

Matthew 4:8-10 NET
Again, the devil took him to a very high mountain, and showed him all the kingdoms of the world and their grandeur.
And he said to him, "I will give you all these things if you throw yourself to the ground and worship me."
Then Jesus said to him, "Go away, Satan! For it is written: 'You are to worship the Lord your God and serve only him.'"

Again, Jesus used scripture, "it is written," to refuse to give in to the deception that he could elevate and gain power for himself. Here we also see the Evil One's overall purpose of wanting to be worshipped as the Most High God.

The Serpent's major tactics are to dazzle and blind a person. He dazzles them with invitations to participate in any kind of counterfeit religion to perpetrate his purposes of deceit. Then the person is blinded to the lies associated with those beliefs. Lies are his biggest weapon. A statement that is not the whole truth is a lie. The Lord Jesus Christ himself called the Evil One the father or originator of lies (John 8:44).

Principality	Devices (Purposes)	Tactics (Methods)	Weapons
Serpent	Deceive, Blind	"Dazzle and blind"	Counterfeit religion, lies, occult, witchcraft

The principality of the Serpent uses the occult and all kinds of sorcery to blind people. The occult has many areas which give people power, but every type of sorcery uses devil spirits to accomplish the "signs and wonders." An example is a medium who predicts the future. He or she must use evil power and familiar spirits to know anything about a person. The occult would include palmistry, tarot cards, hypnosis, levitation and astrology, to name only a few. Any method of seeking supernatural knowledge, guidance and power other than from the true God is included in the term "occult."

There is divination and witchcraft at work in the Church. The Serpent uses false prophecies and visions to speak things which do not come from God. An example occurred at the time of Ezekiel, when the prophets were giving false visions that Jerusalem would remain in peace.

Ezekiel 13:6-9 ESV
They have seen false visions and lying divinations. They say, 'Declares the LORD,' when the LORD has not sent them, and yet they expect him to fulfill their word.
Have you not seen a false vision and uttered a lying divination, whenever you have said, 'Declares the LORD,' although I have not spoken?"
Therefore thus says the Lord GOD: "Because you have uttered falsehood and seen lying visions, therefore behold, I am against you, declares the Lord GOD.
My hand will be against the prophets who see false visions and who give lying divinations. They shall not be in the council of my people, nor be enrolled in the register of the house of Israel, nor shall they enter the land of Israel. And you shall know that I am the Lord GOD.

Although "witchcraft" brings to mind the picture of an old, crooked woman stooped over a cauldron, it is actually a very prevalent form of manipulation found in churches, marriages, and the workplace. Witchcraft, described in the Bible as divination, is sorcery which uses evil spirits to charm or manipulate people.

PRACTICAL APPLICATION

Using the living Word of God as the truth in application is the way to thrust and parry the sword of the Spirit to be effective against any lies of the Serpent. The word that comes from our mouths acts as a sharp sword to divide thoughts and intentions. The sword is used in close combat and must be kept sharpened.

The life of Jesus Christ provides many examples of how the sword of the Spirit is to be used. The Scribes and Pharisees, as religious leaders, had been deceived by the Serpent. They used their religious righteousness to justify their rage at Jesus for not maintaining their traditions. When the Scribes and Pharisees accused Jesus of dishonoring the Law, he pointed out that they had manufactured the oral law to be added to the Mosaic Law. Jesus used the living application of the scriptures to show that they had been deceived.

Matthew 15:1-9 KJV
Then came to Jesus scribes and Pharisees, which were of Jerusalem, saying,
Why do thy disciples transgress the tradition of the elders? for they wash not their hands when they eat bread.
But he answered and said unto them, Why do ye also transgress the commandment of God by your tradition?
For God commanded, saying, Honour thy father and mother: and, He that curseth father or mother, let him die the death.
But ye say, Whosoever shall say to his father or his mother, It is a gift, by whatsoever thou mightest be profited by me;
And honour not his father or his mother, he shall be free. Thus have ye made the commandment of God of none effect by your tradition.
Ye hypocrites, well did Esaias prophesy of you, saying,

This people draweth nigh unto me with their mouth, and honoureth me with their lips; but their heart is far from me.
But in vain they do worship me, teaching for doctrines the commandments of men.

Jesus used exact quotations from the Old Testament to show how the Pharisees were wrong. They had made a law that if someone gave a gift, "Corban" (Mark 7:11) to the temple, he would then not need to care for his father and mother. Jesus distinguishes the truth from the lies just as he did during the temptations in the wilderness.

In the Church, the deceit of the Serpent is not always easy to see. We are not wrestling against flesh and blood, yet there are real people who are speaking lies and half-truths. How do we distinguish what is true? In Acts 16, when Paul and Silas were in Philippi, a girl was following after them speaking things that were actually true. But there was something about the situation that was manipulative. The girl was calling attention to herself, rather than to the words that Paul and Silas were speaking.

Acts 16:16-18 APNT
And it happened that while we were going to the house of prayer, a certain young woman met us who had a spirit of divinations. And she earned a large profit for her masters by the divination that she was divining.
And she was following Paul and us and was crying out and saying, "These men are the servants of the Most High God and are declaring to you the way of life."
And so she did many days. And Paul was provoked and said to that spirit, "I command you in the name of Jesus Christ to come out of her." And immediately it went away.

Paul had to seek a spiritual answer (by revelation) as to what was going on. The girl had a spirit of divination called a Python spirit. This type of spirit is a "power" and will be explained more in the next chapter. Its purpose is to stop the spread of the gospel. Paul waited for the exact time to cast out the spirit.

The sword of the Spirit is the **rhema** Word that is applicable in a specific situation. I can vividly recall a personal example where I ministered healing to someone. The person I was ministering to had been prayed for many times and had been continually exhorted to believe the verse, "by his stripes you were healed" (1 Peter 2:24). Yet the healing was still not apparent. God gave me a different verse to share with her from the record of Aeneas, a man who had been lame for eight years. The Aramaic translation has the following phrase in the present tense: "Jesus Christ heals you." When she heard this truth spoken (as had Aeneas), the words went straight into her heart and she was able to appropriate her healing.

Acts 9:34 APNT
And Simon said to him, "Aeneas, Jesus Christ heals you. Rise up and smooth out your pallet." And immediately he rose up.

No matter what lie is perpetrated in a situation, there is a living Word that is the specific answer and application. It does not matter what kind of deceit there is, the appropriate use of the sword can pierce through to the crux of the matter and bring victory.

CONCLUSION

Below is a chart that summarizes all of the pieces of the armor and how they work to provide complete protection and spiritual clothing for the believer.

PIECE OF ARMOR	HOW ARMOR WORKS
Belt	God's faithfulness to his Word is the source of our strength.
Breastplate	God's legal requirement for justice is met in Jesus Christ; this protects the heart and vital organs.
Sandals	Everyone has a place in the body of Christ, which brings peace and is a firm platform to stand upon.
Shield	The name of Jesus Christ and the nine manifestations of the Spirit extinguish specific attacks.
Helmet	Redemption now and in the future protects our mind.
Sword	The living Word, "it is written," can be used in any situation to separate truth from lies.

Chapter 12
THE POWERS THAT BE

We have looked at all the pieces of the armor and how they are to be utilized. Now we will discuss the second rank of the army of the Evil One: the "powers." In both Greek and Aramaic, this means "one who is in authority." I have compared the powers to the Roman army tribunes, who could work under one or another of the legates (principalities). One group of powers who specialize in lying, for example, can either work for Beelzebub or the Serpent or any of the other principalities. I am presenting this section separately so that the information can be studied as a unit.

In the Pentecostal churches, especially those who specialize in deliverance ministry, these powers or authorities are called "strong men." There have been many books written about spiritual warfare that have endeavored to categorize these evil spirits. A notable classic is *Pigs in the Parlor* by Bill Hammond. Another book I have studied extensively is *Who Are the Strong Men of Our Nation* by Betty Green Suddreth. The powers mentioned in the following chapter are the ones I am certain of – potentially there may be others, as noted by other scholars.

The strong man analogy comes from the section about Beelzebub in Matthew 12 referred to in the chapter on *The Belt of Truth*. The strong man is also described in Luke.

Luke 11:21-22 KJV
When a strong man armed keepeth his palace, his goods are in peace: But when a stronger than he shall come upon him, and overcome him, he taketh from him all his armour wherein he trusted, and divideth his spoils.

Jesus is implying that he is the stronger man who has come to disarm the one who was guarding the house and that he will recapture his possessions and divide the spoils. Now he has given us the privilege of using his name to release people from these "strong men."

The only spirits that God names in the Bible are these spiritual powers. The ones listed in this chapter use the phrase, "spirit of..." and that label describes a category of spirits who have authority in a number of different ways underneath the tribunes. It is better to call these spirits what God calls them, AUTHORITIES. Just doing that makes it clearer that they have power in certain areas. The Aramaic word for "power" here is **shalitna** and its verb root means to "bear rule, bear sway, have the mastery, prevail."[41] These spirits bear rule in specific areas.

We will look at the descriptions of these authorities in the Bible and see what types of evil they cause. This chapter is not intended to cover every kind of evil possible. It is an overview to help facilitate understanding of how the Evil One's army works together as a unit. We will also note which principalities seem to use these tribunes the most. Then we will know which piece(s) of the armor are crucial to defeating these authorities. I have also included specific antidotes and verses that show how to put on the piece of armor needed against each authority.

1. Spirit of Lying (Deceit)

Spirits that work in this authority cause deception, superstition, fraud, false teaching, profanity, hypocrisy and gossip.

1 Kings 22:21-22 NASB
"Then a spirit came forward and stood before the LORD and said, 'I will entice him.'
"And the LORD said to him, 'How?' And he said, 'I will go out and be a deceiving spirit in the mouth of all his prophets.' Then He said, 'You are to entice him and also prevail. Go and do so.'

---

[41] Payne Smith, *A Compendious Syriac Dictionary,* p. 579.

114

Psalm 120:2 NASB
Deliver my soul, O LORD, from lying lips, From a deceitful tongue.

John 8:44 KJV
Ye are of your father the devil, and the lusts of your father ye will do. He was a murderer from the beginning, and abode not in the truth, because there is no truth in him. When he speaketh a lie, he speaketh of his own: for he is a liar, and the father of it.

Proverbs 12:22 ESV
Lying lips are an abomination to the LORD, but those who act faithfully are his delight.

Lying is a major weapon of the Evil One and it is used primarily by Beelzebub and the Serpent.

The antidote to lying is to hold fast to the faithfulness and truth of God's Word, in both written and spoken communication (put on both the belt and the sword).

Ephesians 4:25 KJV
Wherefore putting away lying, speak every man truth with his neighbour: for we are members one of another.

2. Spirit of Perversities (Iniquity)

Spirits that work in this authority cause idolatry, atheism, heresies, sex perversions, sadism, masochism and filthiness.

Isaiah 19:14 KJV
The LORD hath mingled a perverse spirit in the midst thereof: and they have caused Egypt to err in every work thereof, as a drunken man staggereth in his vomit.

A perverse spirit is one that is crooked and does distorted things, referred to in King James Version as "iniquity." In Exodus 34:7, God declares that he visits iniquity to the third and fourth generation. Many times Israel turned to worship other gods of their neighboring nations and adopted their perverse customs. Baal worship was the worst of all, primarily because of the sexual perversion that accompanied it.

Jeremiah 11:10 ESV
They have turned back to the iniquities of their forefathers, who refused to hear my words. They have gone after other gods to serve them. The house of Israel and the house of Judah have broken my covenant that I made with their fathers.

Many times we read in God's Word of the iniquity and idolatry of Israel and think, "Well, at least I am not tempted in that area!" But in our culture, self is the biggest idol, and it has replaced the images of the past with a more subtle form of idolatry. Anything that we put before God is an idol: prestige, position, or popularity.

Both Beelzebub and Belial use this authority frequently.

The antidote to any kind of idolatry is to recognize that God has provided all we have and all we are through our Lord Jesus Christ. He is our source of strength, not ourselves, and is to be relied upon in every situation. We are now made alive in Christ! And the truth of the Word is our standing and position.

Ephesians 2:1-3 KJV
And you hath he quickened, who were dead in trespasses and sins;
Wherein in time past ye walked according to the course of this world, according to the prince of the power of the air, the spirit that now worketh in the children of disobedience:
Among whom also we all had our conversation in times past in the lusts of our flesh, fulfilling the desires of the flesh and of the mind; and were by nature the children of wrath, even as others

3. Spirit of Error (Wandering)

Spirits that work in this authority cause greed, lack of submissiveness, foolishness, oppression, lustful desires, false teaching, deceit, legalism, control, manipulation and rebellion.

1 John 4:6 ESV
We are from God. Whoever knows God listens to us; whoever is not
from God does not listen to us. By this we know the Spirit of truth and
the spirit of error.

This kind of error is a wandering away from the correct application
of the Word. It includes being unteachable, resisting fellowship with
others, greed, love of money, oppression, and what the King James
Version calls "concupiscence," which is "a desire for what is
forbidden." Balaam is an example of someone who used this wrong
behavior to gain something. He was a "prophet for profit." He wanted
to get a monetary reward from King Balak for cursing Israel and was
determined to prophesy against Israel. God stymied his efforts and he
was not able to complete his mission (Numbers 22:4-24:15).

Jude 1:11 KJV
Woe unto them! for they have gone in the way of Cain, and ran
greedily after the error of Balaam for reward, and perished in the
gainsaying of Core.

This authority causes deceit by way of false teaching and rebellion
against God. Sometimes it is called the spirit of antichrist, but that is
not a phrase used in the New Testament. However, one in this state
of deception is an adversary to Christ. I believe that Jezebel is an
example of a person who used this authority to gain control over the
whole kingdom of Israel.

This authority is often used by the Dragon and the Serpent.

One specific antidote is to submit to one another in love and to
cultivate our relationship with God and our brothers and sisters with
thankfulness.

Ephesians 5:20-21 APNT
And give thanks always for everyone in the name of our Lord Jesus
Christ to God the Father.
And be subject to one another in the love of Christ.

4. Spirit of Slumber (Blindness)

Spirits that work in this authority cause blindness, stubbornness, hardness of heart, offense and darkened understanding.

Romans 11:8 NASB
Just as it is written, "God gave them a spirit of stupor, Eyes to see not and ears to hear not, Down to this very day."

Isaiah 29:10 KJV
For the LORD hath poured out upon you the spirit of deep sleep, and hath closed your eyes: the prophets and your rulers, the seers hath he covered.

1 Samuel 15:20-23 KJV
And Saul said unto Samuel, Yea, I have obeyed the voice of the LORD, and have gone the way which the LORD sent me, and have brought Agag the king of Amalek, and have utterly destroyed the Amalekites. But the people took of the spoil, sheep and oxen, the chief of the things which should have been utterly destroyed, to sacrifice unto the LORD thy God in Gilgal.
And Samuel said, Hath the LORD as great delight in burnt offerings and sacrifices, as in obeying the voice of the LORD? Behold, to obey is better than sacrifice, and to hearken than the fat of rams.
For rebellion is as the sin of witchcraft, and stubbornness is as iniquity and idolatry. Because thou hast rejected the word of the LORD, he hath also rejected thee from being king.

Samuel records that Saul closed his ears to the Word of God and that he was rejected because of his stubbornness. Often someone under this authority blames others for their own problems. When Saul was questioned by Samuel about why he did not kill all the Amalekites, Saul blamed the people. This resulted in the kingdom being taken away from Saul. In addition, because Saul allowed King Agag to live, another Amalekite named Haman almost destroyed Israel again in the time of Esther (Esther 8).

This authority is used often by the Dragon and the Serpent.
One antidote is to obey the Word, for the Word brings light and
dispels the darkness.

Ephesians 5:13-17 ESV
But when anything is exposed by the light, it becomes visible,
for anything that becomes visible is light. Therefore it says, "Awake,
O sleeper, and arise from the dead, and Christ will shine on you."
Look carefully then how you walk, not as unwise but as wise,
making the best use of the time, because the days are evil.
Therefore do not be foolish, but understand what the will of the Lord
is.

5. Spirit of Jealousy

Spirits that work in this authority cause envy, hatred, unforgiveness,
revenge, anger, violence, rage, prejudice and murder.

Proverbs 6:34 KJV
For jealousy is the rage of a man: therefore he will not spare in the
day of vengeance.

Proverbs 14:30 KJV
A sound heart is the life of the flesh: but envy [jealousy] the rottenness
of the bones.

Other key verses: Numbers 5:14-31.

This authority is often used by the Dragon and Belial.

A specific antidote is to remember that every person has a place in
the body of Christ, and to let the peace of God be the bond of
completeness.

Ephesians 4:1-3 KJV
I therefore, the prisoner of the Lord, beseech you that ye walk worthy
of the vocation wherewith ye are called,

With all lowliness and meekness, with longsuffering, forbearing one another in love;
Endeavouring to keep the unity of the Spirit in the bond of peace.

Colossians 3:15 KJV
And let the peace of God rule in your hearts, to the which also ye are called in one body; and be ye thankful.

6. Spirit of Haughtiness (Pride)

Spirits that work in this authority cause contentions, judgmental criticism, scorning, self-righteousness, self-pity, wars, manipulation and control.

Proverbs 16:18-19 KJV
Pride goeth before destruction, and an haughty spirit before a fall. Better it is to be of an humble spirit with the lowly, than to divide the spoil with the proud.

Job 41 is a description of Leviathan, which is a giant sea monster used to depict what pride is. He has scales of armor that are almost impossible to penetrate.

Job 41:12-17, 34 KJV
I will not conceal his parts, nor his power, nor his comely proportion.
Who can discover the face of his garment? or who can come to him with his double bridle?
Who can open the doors of his face? his teeth are terrible round about.
His scales are his pride, shut up together as with a close seal.
One is so near to another, that no air can come between them.
They are joined one to another, they stick together, that they cannot be sundered.

Other key verses: 1 Timothy 6:3-6.

This authority is often used by the Dragon and Beelzebub.

One antidote to pride is kindness and compassion.

Titus 3:3-6 APNT
For we were also previously without sense and we were disobedient and we were erring and we were serving various passions and we were occupied with wickedness and with envy and we were being hateful. We were even hating one another.
But when the kindness and compassion of God, our Life-giver, was revealed,
not by works of justification that we did, but by his own mercies, he gave us life by the washing of the birth from above and by the renewing of the Holy Spirit,
which he poured out on us abundantly by way of Jesus Christ, our Life-giver.

Another practical way to deny pride any foothold in your life is found in Proverbs.

Proverbs 30:32 NASB
If you have been foolish in exalting yourself or if you have plotted evil, put your hand on your mouth.

7. Spirit of Fear

Spirits that work in this authority cause anxiety, torment, phobias, compulsive behavior patterns, insomnia, terror, anguish, nightmares, fear of rejection and all fears.

2 Timothy 1:7 KJV
For God hath not given us the spirit of fear; but of power, and of love, and of a sound mind.

Fear causes torment in the mind and soul of a person; it causes one to freeze and to be unable to move. Therefore it is used most often by Satan. God's Word has many records of exhortations not to fear. Genesis 15 is the first occurence.

Genesis 15:1 ESV
After these things the word of the LORD came to Abram in a vision:
"Fear not, Abram, I am your shield; your reward shall be very
great."

One specific antidote to fear is putting on the love that God has for
us. He will never leave or forsake us.

1 John 4:18 ESV
There is no fear in love, but perfect love casts out fear. For fear has
to do with punishment, and whoever fears has not been perfected in
love.

8. Spirit of Bondage

Spirits that work in this authority cause addictions, captivity of every
kind, bitterness and shame.

Romans 8:15 APNT
For you have not received the spirit of bondage again to fear, but you
have received the Spirit of adoption by which we call, "Father, our
Father."

Proverbs 5:22 ESV
The iniquities of the wicked ensnare him, and he is held fast in the
cords of his sin.

2 Timothy 2:26 ESV
and they may come to their senses and escape from the snare of the
devil, after being captured by him to do his will.

Other key verses: 2 Peter 2:18-20.

This authority is used often by Belial and the Devil.

One specific antidote is walking in our relationship with God as sons.

Galatians 4:3-9 KJV
Even so we, when we were children, were in bondage under the
elements of the world:
But when the fulness of the time was come, God sent forth his Son,
made of a woman, made under the law,
To redeem them that were under the law, that we might receive the
adoption of sons.
And because ye are sons, God hath sent forth the Spirit of his Son into
your hearts, crying, Abba, Father.
Wherefore thou art no more a servant, but a son; and if a son, then
an heir of God through Christ.
Howbeit then, when ye knew not God, ye did service unto them which
by nature are no gods.
But now, after that ye have known God, or rather are known of God,
how turn ye again to the weak and beggarly elements, whereunto ye
desire again to be in bondage?

9. Spirit of Divination

Spirits that work in this authority use familiar spirits, the occult, astrology, fortunetelling, spiritualism and idolatry.

Leviticus 20:27 NASB
"Now a man or a woman who is a medium or a spiritist shall surely
be put to death. They shall be stoned with stones, their bloodguiltiness
is upon them."

In the Old Testament, using divination was a capital offense. As noted before, in Acts Paul dealt with a slave girl who was following him in Philippi and using divination. This spirit is called a Python spirit and can work against the spread of the gospel in a church or area. Its main way of attacking is to grab hold of a person and squeeze the life out of them.

Acts 16:16 ESV
As we were going to the place of prayer, we were met by a slave girl
who had a spirit of divination and brought her owners much gain by
fortune-telling.

This authority is used by the Devil and the Serpent.

One specific antidote to this authority is to do what God instructed Israel to do: drive them out. When Israel went in to possess the Promised Land, they needed to get rid of the witches and wizards. The reason for this was that the counterfeit is often very difficult to tell from the truth.

Deuteronomy 18:9-12 KJV
When thou art come into the land which the LORD thy God giveth thee, thou shalt not learn to do after the abominations of those nations.
There shall not be found among you any one that maketh his son or his daughter to pass through the fire, or that useth divination, or an observer of times, or an enchanter, or a witch,
Or a charmer, or a consulter with familiar spirits, or a wizard, or a necromancer.
For all that do these things are an abomination unto the LORD: and because of these abominations the LORD thy God doth drive them out from before thee.

10. Spirit of Whoredom

Spirits that use this authority cause fornication, adultery (can be spiritual adultery), lust and prostitution.

Hosea 4:12 ESV
My people inquire of a piece of wood, and their walking staff gives them oracles. For a spirit of whoredom has led them astray, and they have left their God to play the whore.

Whoredom means fornication or prostitution. Israel continued to play with worshipping other gods besides Yahweh and gave the dominion to another "lord." Beelzebub predominantly uses this authority, but Belial also uses it to capture people in sexual lusts.

Hebrews 12:16 KJV
Lest there be any fornicator, or profane person, as Esau, who for one morsel of meat sold his birthright.

Esau is given as an example of someone who "profaned" or despised his birth as the eldest son, married two Canaanite women (which would have polluted the Christ line), and then sold his birthright to Jacob.

A specific antidote is to be washed, sanctified and justified. We are washed spiritually, but because of daily sins we can also be washed every day.

I Corinthians 6:9-12 KJV
Know ye not that the unrighteous shall not inherit the kingdom of God? Be not deceived: neither fornicators, nor idolaters, nor adulterers, nor effeminate, nor abusers of themselves with mankind, Nor thieves, nor covetous, nor drunkards, nor revilers, nor extortioners, shall inherit the kingdom of God.
And such were some of you: but ye are washed, but ye are sanctified, but ye are justified in the name of the Lord Jesus, and by the Spirit of our God.
All things are lawful unto me, but all things are not expedient: all things are lawful for me, but I will not be brought under the power of any.

11. Spirit of Infirmity

Spirits that work under this authority cause chronic illnesses of every kind, including cancer, auto-immune diseases and mental illness.

Luke 13:11-13 APNT
There was a woman there who had had a spirit of infirmity [for] eighteen years and she was bent over and was not able to straighten at all.
And Jesus saw her and called her and said to her, "Woman, you are free from your infirmity."

And he placed his hand on her and immediately she straightened and praised God.

The King James Version says "loosed from your infirmity." She needed to be set free from what was holding her in this chronic condition. The length of her sickness had built a weakness or infirmity in her and thereby incapacitated her. This is the case with most chronic conditions. That is why this authority is used most often by Satan to cause great bondage and fear.

Some deliverance ministries separate out the "deaf and dumb spirit" and make it a separate "power." They include mental illness under this dumb spirit. The best approach is to call both physical and mental illness the work of spirits of infirmity.

The antidote is to use the power behind the name of Jesus Christ to set the person free. Jesus commanded the ears of the deaf man to be opened as the example of dealing with this authority.

Mark 7:32-35 APNT
And they brought him a certain deaf man, a stammerer, and were asking him to place a hand on him.
And he led him away from the crowd privately and placed his fingers in his ears and he spit and touched his tongue.
And he looked into heaven and sighed and said to him, "Be opened."
And immediately his ears were opened and the restriction of his tongue was loosed and he spoke plainly.

12. Spirit of Heaviness

Spirits under this authority cause grief, despair, depression, hopelessness, gloominess, rejection, loneliness and faintness of heart and mind.

Isaiah 61:3 KJV
To appoint unto them that mourn in Zion, to give unto them beauty for ashes, the oil of joy for mourning, the garment of praise for the

spirit of heaviness; that they might be called trees of righteousness, the planting of the LORD, that he might be glorified.

The New American Standard Version calls this authority "the spirit of fainting" because it causes people to be so weary that they give up. For example, a dimness of the mind happens when grief or despair takes over. Heaviness could also come from outside circumstances, as with Paul in Asia. Paul was so pressed that he despaired of continuing to live.

2 Corinthians 1:8 KJV
For we would not, brethren, have you ignorant of our trouble which came to us in Asia, that we were pressed out of measure, above strength, insomuch that we despaired even of life:

This authority is used most often by Belial and the Devil.

The antidote is stated in Isaiah 61:3 – put on "the garment of praise." The Old Testament contains many examples of battles against tremendous odds, when God told the leaders to send out musicians or singers first. The battle lead by Jehoshaphat in 2 Chronicles 20 is one such example.

Paul wrote Philippians when he was in bonds in Rome, but he tells the Philippians that he will continue to rejoice no matter what.

Philippians 1:12-20 KJV
But I would ye should understand, brethren, that the things which happened unto me have fallen out rather unto the furtherance of the gospel;
So that my bonds in Christ are manifest in all the palace, and in all other places;
And many of the brethren in the Lord, waxing confident by my bonds, are much more bold to speak the word without fear.
Some indeed preach Christ even of envy and strife; and some also of good will:
The one preach Christ of contention, not sincerely, supposing to add affliction to my bonds:

But the other of love, knowing that I am set for the defence of the gospel.
What then? notwithstanding, every way, whether in pretence, or in truth, Christ is preached; and I therein do rejoice, yea, and will rejoice.
For I know that this shall turn to my salvation through your prayer, and the supply of the Spirit of Jesus Christ,
According to my earnest expectation and my hope, that in nothing I shall be ashamed, but that with all boldness, as always, so now also Christ shall be magnified in my body, whether it be by life, or by death.

SUMMARY

Once we can identify by revelation the "tribune" (power) in charge, it becomes very clear what to do, either to heal an area of our own lives or to minister to someone else. We could possibly write an entire book expanding on this chapter. But once we recognize the rank of these authorities and how they work together with other spirits in the army of the Evil One, his strategy is exposed.

Jesus said in John 10:10 that the "thief comes not but for to steal, kill and destroy." All six principalities are covered in this statement. If a house is broken into, it needs to be repaired, rebuilt, restored or replaced. Healing from spiritual attacks requires these same repairs. Once the designs of these authorities are exposed (as we have done), we can walk according to the Spirit and learn what needs to be done to repair a person's house. There are no methods as far as what to do in these situations. Each and every circumstance requires fresh revelation from God. Our victory has been won by our Lord Jesus Christ. Let's put on the whole armor of God and stand together in that victory!

Chapter 13
CASTING DOWN STRONGHOLDS

God has given us the weapons of the armor of God and our spiritual clothing so we can overcome and pull down strongholds of thinking that are contrary to Christ. In order to put on the new man and utilize the armor of God, we also need to strip off the old man. Every believer comes to Christ with certain mindsets based on misinformation and these do not automatically get corrected, even by scripturally correct teaching. These strongholds of thinking need to be cast down. So what is a stronghold?

A stronghold is a place that has been fortified to protect against attack. It is essentially a defensive structure. David had many strongholds that he used to hide his men from King Saul's pursuit and he also called God his "fortress."

Psalm 18:2 NET
The LORD is my high ridge, my stronghold, my deliverer. My God is my rocky summit where I take shelter, my shield, the horn that saves me, and my refuge.

The Hebrew word for "stronghold" is **metsudah.** Herod built the fortress city of Masada on top of a huge mountain near the Dead Sea and called it "the fortress." Man erects fortresses out of stone or brick to protect himself from external dangers, but he also builds thinking patterns which act in the same way. A stronghold is whatever people delight in, "their joy and glory."

Ezekiel 24:25 ESV
As for you, son of man, surely on the day when I take from them their stronghold, their joy and glory, the delight of their eyes and their soul's desire, and also their sons and daughters,

Strongholds can originate in our own minds and imaginations or come from our environment and relationships. A stronghold is what one uses to fortify and defend a personal belief, idea or opinion against outside opposition. It is the fortification around and defense of what we believe.[42] We should look for the presence of a stronghold when we find ourselves powerless to change a situation that is contrary to the will of God.[43] For example, we are to forgive our enemies; that is obviously the will of God. So when we are unable to forgive a particular person, we must look for the stronghold of thinking that needs to be cast down.

2 Corinthians 10:4-5 APNT
For the equipment of our service is not of the flesh, but of the power of God and by it, we overcome rebellious strongholds.
And we pull down reasonings and all pride that elevates [itself] against the knowledge of God and we lead captive all thoughts to the obedience of Christ.

The "equipment of our service" in other translations is "the weapons of our warfare." The Greek word for "stronghold" is only used here in 2 Corinthians and means "anything on which one relies." The Aramaic word has to do with what is stored up (in our thinking), and a related noun means "treasure." What we treasure and store up in our minds – a habit of thinking we rely on – can be a good stronghold (that protects us) or a "rebellious stronghold" that will defeat us if we do not pull it down. The Hebrew word picture is that of a cooking pot with deposits in it that will not be burned off or go away.

A noun in Aramaic related to the verb "overcome" is **kuvsha,** which means "footstool." We need to learn to put all false reasoning and pride under our feet. James Murdock, who translated the Peshitta New Testament in 1861, translated the phrase "lead captive all thoughts" as "subjugating all reasonings."

---

[42] Liberty Savard, *Shattering Your Strongholds*, p. 28.
[43] Ed Silvoso, *That None Should Perish,* p. 159.

CASTING DOWN STRONGHOLDS

2 Corinthians 10:5 MRD
And we demolish imaginations, and every lofty thing that exalteth itself against the knowledge of God, and subjugate all reasonings to obedience to the Messiah.

Our reasonings are thought patterns that become engrained in our minds. God knows all about strongholds and he will tell us how to overcome them and cast them down – if we are willing to fight!

There are three steps to dealing with negative strongholds:

1. Identify the pattern
2. Cast down the false reasoning
3. Obey the word of Christ

We have learned about the six principalities and their tactics. I want to use this framework to present examples of how to accomplish these steps. Remember that when the Evil One is exposed, we are on the way to standing in victory!

Principality	Identify Pattern	Cast Down	Obey
Beelzebub	Idol or grove of idols	False worship	Repair the temple and change your words to line up with God's Word
Devil	Wounds in the heart	Condemnation, Resentment	Cleanse and bandage the wounds with forgiveness
Dragon	Source of Pride	Comparison	Become a servant with meekness

Satan	Kind of fear	Panic	Claim what is yours with authority, lock shields with others
Belial	Perversity	Rebellion, Rejection	Obey a positive way of living, grasp hope for the future
Serpent	Deception	Lies	Decree and apply specific verses of truth

Each of the following subtitles has to do with the principalities in the chart above.

WHO IS LORD?

Beelzebub promotes strongholds of thinking that have to do with who or what is Lord in our lives.

Josiah was a king of Judah who began his reign at 8 years old. His father Amon and grandfather Manasseh had departed from worshipping God and had set up groves to Baal throughout the land. When Josiah was 16 years old, he began to purge the idols and he broke down the altars and the images.

2 Chronicles 34:3-4 KJV
For in the eighth year of his reign, while he was yet young, he began to seek after the God of David his father: and in the twelfth year he began to purge Judah and Jerusalem from the high places, and the groves, and the carved images, and the molten images.
And they brake down the altars of Baalim in his presence; and the images, that were on high above them, he cut down; and the groves, and the carved images, and the molten images, he brake in pieces,

and made dust of them, and strowed it upon the graves of them that had sacrificed unto them.

Josiah was committed to the long-term purging of the land. When he was 26 he began to repair the temple. After all the repairs were complete, he reestablished the reading of the Law and the people repented of their false worship.

2 Chronicles 34:30-33 KJV
And the king went up into the house of the LORD, and all the men of Judah, and the inhabitants of Jerusalem, and the priests, and the Levites, and all the people, great and small: and he read in their ears all the words of the book of the covenant that was found in the house of the LORD.
And the king stood in his place, and made a covenant before the LORD, to walk after the LORD, and to keep his commandments, and his testimonies, and his statutes, with all his heart, and with all his soul, to perform the words of the covenant which are written in this book.
And he caused all that were present in Jerusalem and Benjamin to stand to it. And the inhabitants of Jerusalem did according to the covenant of God, the God of their fathers.
And Josiah took away all the abominations out of all the countries that pertained to the children of Israel, and made all that were present in Israel to serve, even to serve the LORD their God. And all his days they departed not from following the LORD, the God of their fathers.

This example shows how to tear down a mental stronghold. The idols need to be identified and then torn down. The temple needs to be repaired. Then the true lordship and worship of God must be established by lining up our thinking with the Word of God.

A modern example of tearing down a stronghold comes from a time when my family and I were living in New Mexico. One stronghold of thinking in that part of the country came partially from the dominance of American Indian tribes and their spiritual practices and the land was overrun with poverty. We ministered to a particular tribe who lived on a reservation outside of Albuquerque. The people there barely survived on the pittance of a handout from the government. Deep hopelessness was evident. There was no money to build adequate housing, and food was scarce. There was little motivation to work hard or to try to change anything; the prevalent thought was, "What's the use?" How did we help them begin to tear down the stronghold? By encouraging the women on the reservation to make baskets and other household items and sell them. Gradually their thinking was changed and they began to make a good living. The patterns of hopelessness were torn down and replaced with the truth of the Word that "my God shall supply all your need" (Philippians 4:19).

We need to identify patterns of thinking that are engrained in our minds and then cast down the reasoning. The temple of our mind needs to be repaired and then restored with the promises of God's faithfulness. Only after that will we be able to walk in freedom and true worship.

WHERE ARE THE WOUNDS?

The Devil tries to develop strongholds of thinking that have to do with condemnation and deep wounds.

In order to be healed from condemnation and hurts that have come from slander or accusation, the wounds in the heart need to be identified. Then we need to cast down any kind of resentment harbored against someone that has lodged in the heart and fortified it against being hurt again.

A fellow minister told me of a vision she received which I believe is very powerful. She saw "wounds of the heart" that had been buried in a cemetery and had tombstones erected to memorialize them. The wounds were buried, but unlike a dead body, they continued to fester and boil under the earth. Not only did the wound need to be unburied and have forgiveness applied to it, but the tombstone needed to be pushed over and broken into tiny pieces so that there was no longer a memorial to the wound.

Jesus came to heal the broken-hearted with forgiveness and to further set the captives free. He summarized his whole mission at the beginning of his ministry by quoting Isaiah 61:1 and Isaiah 58:6.

Luke 4:18 APNT
The Spirit of the LORD [is] on me and because of this, he has anointed me to preach to the poor and has sent me to heal the broken-hearted and to preach forgiveness to the captives and sight to the blind and to strengthen the broken with forgiveness.

In order for a person to be healed of a physical wound or cut, the cut first needs to be cleansed. If the cut is deep, it needs to be sewn up or cauterized. Then ointment or salve can be applied to the wound and it can be bandaged. Once a cut is healed, there may be a scar, but there is no further pain. The same process applies to dressing wounds in our soul.

Corrie ten Boom was a Christian woman who, along with her father and family, hid Jews in their house in the Netherlands during World War II. After several years they were discovered. Corrie and her sister Betsy were sent to the concentration camp in Ravensbruck. A specific guard had harassed all the women by ogling and taunting them as he watched them shower. He had been savagely cruel to Corrie's sister and had played a part in her death. Corrie survived the camp, but after her release she had no family left. In the camp she had encouraged others to rely on God and forgive their tormentors; now she decided to preach a message of forgiveness and restoration. She did this for many years. One time when she was preaching, she looked out into the audience and saw the guard who had been instrumental in her sister's death.

The man came up to her at the end of the service and explained that he was now a Christian. He asked Corrie if she could find it in her heart to forgive him. That was a turning point for Corrie because although she felt she had forgiven the atrocities she had suffered, the wound and resentment about her sister's death had remained. She managed to cry out to God for help with forgiving the man and silently grasped his hand. "You are forgiven," she said. And at that moment she was set free.[44]

When wounds have occurred over a long period of time, especially in childhood, the process of healing may take time. I know of a man who had a very abusive father who beat him and verbally shamed him his whole childhood. Once he became a Christian, he forgave his father but had trouble picturing God as a loving Father. There needed to be much bandaging and receiving the loving salve of compassion to release the expectation that as soon as he did something wrong, he would be punished for it.

Wounds of the heart must be identified and all resentment and hurt cast down. Then the love of God can heal and soothe the broken-heartedness and set the person free.

ME – PRIDEFUL?

The Dragon tries to develop strongholds of thinking via pride, stubbornness, and jealousy.

If someone thinks they are not prideful, that is the first problem. No one is exempt from being attacked in this area. After the fall the first thing Adam and Eve did was try to take care of themselves by sewing together fig leaves for clothing. Every person since that time has had to deal with the same tendency – to meet their own needs rather than relying on God to take care of them.

Israel is described as being prideful. They did not listen to or obey God's commandments. Nehemiah describes how they built this stronghold of thinking to a point where they were not allowed to go into the Promised Land. Note how they hardened their necks and became stubborn.

---

[44] David Jeremiah, *Slaying the Giants in Your Life,* pp. 132-133.

CASTING DOWN STRONGHOLDS

Nehemiah 9:16-17 KJV
But they and our fathers dealt proudly, and hardened their necks, and
hearkened not to thy commandments,
And refused to obey, neither were mindful of thy wonders that thou
didst among them; but hardened their necks, and in their rebellion
appointed a captain to return to their bondage: but thou art a God
ready to pardon, gracious and merciful, slow to anger, and of great
kindness, and forsookest them not.

The children of Israel were not mindful of the wonders that God had
done among them, such as the plagues that afflicted the Egyptians,
the parting of the Red Sea, providing water out of the rock, and
feeding them with manna. This led to a stubbornness that finally
issued in rebelling and wanting to go back to Egypt. The only ones of
the older generation who were allowed into the Promised Land were
Joshua and Caleb, because they believed that God would fight the
battles for them if they obeyed his commandments.

The source of pride must first be identified. This is clear in another
example of pride in the life of King Saul. Here we can see a vivid
illustration of where envy and comparison leads. When David
became known for his battles with the Philistines, Saul began to be
angry and very jealous.

I Samuel 18:7-9 KJV
And the women answered one another as they played, and said, Saul
hath slain his thousands, and David his ten thousands.
And Saul was very wroth, and the saying displeased him; and he said,
They have ascribed unto David ten thousands, and to me they have
ascribed but thousands: and what can he have more but the kingdom?
And Saul eyed David from that day and forward.

The New Living Translation of verse 9 says that "from that time on
Saul kept a jealous eye on David." The next day he was troubled by
an evil spirit and tried to kill David with a spear.

CASTING DOWN STRONGHOLDS

1 Samuel 18:10-11 ESV
The next day a harmful spirit from God rushed upon Saul, and he raved within his house while David was playing the lyre, as he did day by day. Saul had his spear in his hand.
And Saul hurled the spear, for he thought, "I will pin David to the wall." But David evaded him twice.

Envy led Saul from anger to jealousy to endeavoring to murder David for about nine years. If Saul had identified what led to this stronghold developing in his mind, he would have needed to stop the comparison between himself and David. Saul had become jealous of David because the people, including his son Jonathan, loved David and followed him because he acted wisely (1 Samuel 18:15).

In the present day Church, this scenario of pride plays out when a pastor gets jealous of another elder or youth pastor after comparing himself to his fellow worker's success in working with people. This can turn into a stronghold – an unsound thinking pattern – if the comparison is not cast down and replaced by humility. The obedience needed is to become a servant, as Jesus displayed when he washed the disciple's feet. The applicable truth of the Word is that every member has his own place in the body of Christ and there is room for every member.

DO NOT FEAR WHAT THEY FEAR

Satan promotes strongholds of thinking that foster an inability to do anything to combat fear.

Assyria had conquered and taken northern Israel into captivity and was aggressively conquering all the kingdoms southward to Egypt. The early prophecies of Isaiah protested against the foreign alliances being negotiated by Israel with Syria and Samaria. He specifically warned King Ahaz of Judah against the dangers involved in an alliance with Assyria. The heads of two puppet kingdoms (Syria and northern Israel) asked King Ahaz to join with them in a coalition against Assyria. When Ahaz refused, they threatened to make war

138

against him. Isaiah received revelation to prophesy to the people not to fear what others were fearing.

Isaiah 8:9-15 ESV
Be broken, you peoples, and be shattered; give ear, all you far countries; strap on your armor and be shattered; strap on your armor and be shattered.
Take counsel together, but it will come to nothing; speak a word, but it will not stand, for God is with us.
For the LORD spoke thus to me with his strong hand upon me, and warned me not to walk in the way of this people, saying:
"Do not call conspiracy all that this people calls conspiracy, and do not fear what they fear, nor be in dread.
But the LORD of hosts, him you shall honor as holy. Let him be your fear, and let him be your dread.
And he will become a sanctuary and a stone of offense and a rock of stumbling to both houses of Israel, a trap and a snare to the inhabitants of Jerusalem.
And many shall stumble on it. They shall fall and be broken; they shall be snared and taken."

Instead of being full of fear, they were to honor and reverence God and rely on his power. But King Ahaz stumbled at this idea; he eventually succumbed and allied Judah with Assyria. About 20 years later, the Assyrian army was on the doorstep of Jerusalem in the time of Hezekiah (Ahaz's son). They were finally routed by a miraculous victory. The whole Assyrian army was defeated in one night and 185,000 were killed by the angel of the Lord (2 Kings 18, 19). Because Hezekiah believed what Isaiah had said, God was a sanctuary for him. King Ahaz and others stumbled at Isaiah's exhortation not to make alliances with the enemy and continued in their fear. This is the choice in all situations of fear. Either we can trust that God will deliver and remain constant in that assurance, or we can try to make substitute alliances that take the place of trust in God.

Fear of man can become a snare or stronghold. When one person exerts control or domination over another for an extended period of time, it can lead to a stronghold of fear in the person being dominated. An example of this is a woman with an abusive husband. If the woman is enabling her husband's behavior, fear that the bruises and physical wounds will be discovered leads the woman to try to hide the fact that abuse is occurring. There is also usually fear that the husband will retaliate if the abuse is exposed.

Proverbs 29:25 ESV
The fear of people becomes a snare, but whoever trusts in the LORD will be set on high.

The process of identification is very important here. What is causing the fear? It could be a devil spirit but there could also be a stronghold associated with the fear. To identify the cause, there must be revelation from God and/or help from others. Each situation is different. The fear must be identified; in this case, part of how to do that is to uncover what is hidden. Then the person needs to be helped to feel safe in a different environment.

I have seen people have panic attacks when they merely think of a certain person. A panic attack is defined in Wikipedia as "a sudden sensation of fear, which is so strong as to dominate or prevent reason and logical thinking, replacing it with overwhelming feelings of anxiety and frantic agitation consistent with an animalistic fight-or-flight reaction."[45] Anyone who has experienced panic of this nature has trouble knowing what caused it. Again, this is a situation where revelation is needed to identify the cause of the fear and help change the pattern of thinking. As we saw in the chapter on *The Shield of the Name of Jesus Christ,* we often need to lock shields with other believers to help win a victory.

REBELLION AND REJECTION

Belial tries to develop strongholds of rebellion and rejection in order to keep someone in bondage.

---

[45] Wikipedia, "panic"

Bondage is caused when a person serves a sin or perversity that is contrary to God's design for life. That person is literally handing over his service and obedience to something perverse such as drugs, homosexuality, pornography, or alcoholism.

Romans 6:16 NET
Do you not know that if you present yourselves as obedient slaves, you are slaves of the one you obey, either of sin resulting in death, or obedience resulting in righteousness?

All these kinds of bondage are rooted in rebellion against the principles set up by God for righteous and holy living. The strongholds of thoughts are "against the knowledge of God" (2 Corinthians 10:5). The perversion needs to be identified – what is crooked and twisted and contrary to God's will. Then the rebellion must be cast down; the walls surrounding thoughts like "I can choose my own lifestyle," or "These habits are not hurting anyone," must be taken apart, stone by stone. Once this is done, God will transform us into a new person.

Romans 12:2 NLT
Don't copy the behavior and customs of this world, but let God transform you into a new person by changing the way you think. Then you will learn to know God's will for you, which is good and pleasing and perfect.

An example of someone in bondage is a person controlled by an eating disorder, such as anorexia or bulimia. A 99 pound woman stands in front of a mirror and sees someone who is fat. Though the fat image is far from true to a casual observer, to that woman the image is very real. I once knew a woman who was enslaved by this type of bondage. She would go on a binge and eat an entire chocolate cake, then try to reverse the effects of the binge by making herself vomit until she was so weak she could not stand. This vicious cycle controlled her for about four years before she was able to overcome the underlying pattern of thinking. She had to identify the perversity as well as the incorrect mindset. She had believed she was unlovable and this had opened her up to the bondage.

Usually, the actual perversity is easy to identify. The rebellion is not. The child who starts smoking cigarettes behind the barn at the age of 12 knows that he is rebelling against his parents and his upbringing. However, the young adult hooked on drugs may not recognize that he is in rebellion against the expectations of God. I was in college during the late 1960's during an era of "free love" and smoking pot and trying all kinds of drugs. These temptations came even at the Christian college I attended. It actually looked like rebellion if someone did **not** want to try drugs!

Rejection is one of the worst and most common wounds of people. Rejection results from the denial of love. If the rejection is not dealt with, a person can succumb to bondage like depression and suicide and the wrong thinking patterns that result. The life of Elijah gives an example of this.

Elijah had spent many years prophesying against Jezebel and the idolatry of Baal worship. At the height of his confrontation with Jezebel, Elijah won a seemingly impossible victory on Mount Carmel when God sent fire to prove that he was greater than Baal. Elijah should have been rejoicing in the victory. However, as soon as Jezebel discovered that all of her prophets had been killed, she sent a note to Elijah to say, "So let the gods do to me, and more also, if I make not thy life as the life of one of them by tomorrow about this time" (1 Kings 19:2). Instead of becoming even more determined to stand up to Jezebel's idolatry, Elijah fled for his life. He went a day's journey into the wilderness and sat under a juniper tree with a serious case of depression. He felt he had been rejected by God and all the people.

1 Kings 19:4 KJV
But he himself went a day's journey into the wilderness, and came and sat down under a juniper tree: and he requested for himself that he might die; and said, It is enough; now, O LORD, take away my life; for I am not better than my fathers.

Even after an angel fed him and he walked all the way to Mount Horeb in forty days, he was still depressed. God worked with him in a miraculous way to give him courage to continue on the path he had for him. God told him that his work was not finished and that there were 7000 in Israel who had not bowed to Baal. That gave Elijah hope! Once Elijah was encouraged, God told him that he was to go and anoint Elisha. Now it was up to him to be obedient to the words God had spoken to him. He obeyed God's instruction and anointed Elisha, who continued to be Elijah's servant for the rest of Elijah's days (2 Kings 3:11).

WHAT ARE THE LIES?

The Serpent fosters strongholds of thinking that direct the thoughts away from the true cause.

Sickness can be from natural causes, but when it is caused by thinking such as self-hate or self-rejection, it is a stronghold of deception. The deception needs to be identified and the lies cast down.

Henry Wright, the author of the book *A More Excellent Way*, has helped many to overcome serious physical and emotional sicknesses. He writes that self-unforgiveness, self-resentment, self-hate, and self-rejection are some of the major sources of autoimmune diseases such as lupus, multiple sclerosis and Crohn's disease. This is how he summarizes his conclusions:

> The body attacks the body because the person is attacking themselves spiritually in self-rejection, self-hatred, and self-bitterness. There is a spiritual dynamic that comes in which the white corpuscles are invisibly redirected to attack living tissue while ignoring the true enemy which are bacteria and viruses.[46]

The deception must be identified by personally realizing it or by help from a deliverance minister or fellow Christian. Then the lies can be

---

[46] www.greatbiblestudy.com/anti-self_bondages.php

refuted by using specific scripture verses. The person needs to apply specific verses of the Word to their situation to stand in victory.

When I was on a mission trip to Romania, a group of seven ministers and I went to a Gypsy village. We noticed something very strange about the village. Normally Gypsies are very exuberant people but in this village there was a sadness everywhere we looked. After settling in, we began playing some music and mingling with the crowd. My pastor noticed that several children were cross-eyed. He began to pray for them and two or three of the children got healed. Suddenly, the people whose houses surrounded the courtyard where we ministered came pouring out of their houses. We were astonished at how many of the children who came into the courtyard were cross-eyed! Before I could comprehend what was happening, a lady walked over to me and thrust her crying baby into my arms. She was excitedly waving her hands and speaking Romanian. I looked around for an interpreter but there was no one available. So I simply started ministering to the baby in English and the baby stopped crying. We found out later that the baby had been crying incessantly for a long time and no one could figure out why. After the crying baby and the cross-eyed children were healed, more and more people lined up in the courtyard to be healed.

After we had ministered for a while, my pastor called us together and informed us that we needed to take a spiritual stand against a witch who was standing at the edge of the crowd and screaming. She was very upset because we were breaking her control in that village. She had put a curse on the children, which was why they were cross-eyed. We prayed and broke her control in the name of Jesus Christ. She backed down and ceased screaming. Eventually she left the community, having been rendered powerless by the power of God. The Romanian pastors continued to minister in this village and many people turned to the Lord.

In this incident we identified the source of the deception (the witch), cast down the lies (that the children would be permanently cross-eyed), and obeyed God's directive to preach and heal all those who are oppressed by the Evil One just like Jesus did (Acts 10:38). The power of witchcraft can set up strongholds which are not of someone's own choosing. This type of situation requires walking by the Spirit and utilizing the name of Jesus Christ as well as identifying the lies.

SUMMARY

Strongholds are wrong thinking patterns. The patterns need to be identified and the stronghold or fortress cast down and overcome. Once the lies and faulty thinking are exposed, only obedience to the truth of the Word will change the thoughts and consequently the actions that follow. The examples given in this chapter are representative of the strongholds that are promoted by each of the principalities.

When he was first crowned king of Israel, David conquered and overcame the stronghold of the city of the Jebusites (which would later become the city of Jerusalem). From the time of Joshua, it had never been captured because it was set high on a mountain and had a fortress wall surrounding it. The people within the city were very confident that no one, including David, could ever take the fortress.

2 Samuel 5:6 NET
Then the king and his men advanced to Jerusalem against the Jebusites who lived in the land. The Jebusites said to David, "You cannot invade this place! Even the blind and the lame will turn you back, saying, 'David cannot invade this place!'"

The Jebusite's taunting and accusation made David even more determined to take the fortress. He did not shrink back in unbelief. Neither was he dismayed because of his ancestor's failures. David looked at the battle in light of God's promises. God had told Abraham, "Your descendants will take possession of the strongholds of their enemies" (Genesis 22:17).

Though the record in God's Word does not give a detailed description of how David and his men did it, he and his men ascended the water shaft which started at the Gihon spring. During my trip to Israel, I saw this water shaft in Jerusalem because it is part of the ongoing excavations of the City of David. God must have shown David what to do; rather than try to attack the stronghold head on, he went through a back door and surprised the Jebusites.

2 Samuel 5:7 NET
But David captured the fortress of Zion (that is, the city of David).

David did not actually tear down the stronghold of Zion, but instead rebuilt it into the capital city of the whole nation. The temple was eventually built there to honor the true God. David tore down the rebellious stronghold and then fortified it in obedience to God.

There is no stronghold that cannot be pulled down when we rely on the faithfulness of God's Word and make it the source of our strength (the belt of truth). God helps us to identify wounds in our hearts and shows us how to deflect the accusations of the Evil One (the breastplate of justification). When faced with stubbornness and pride, seek for God's revelation with meekness and be prepared to be a servant (the sandals of the gospel of peace). Use the authority we have been given in Christ, and cast down any discouragement or possibility of defeat (the shield of faith). Sort out the lies and deception with the application of the living Word (the sword of the Spirit). Then stand with THE ARMOR OF VICTORY!

Chapter 14
BEING PREPARED IN EVERYTHING, STAND

There are many resources available for further study on the topic of spiritual warfare. I encourage you to peruse the bibliography containing the books which have enlightened me in this study. Many testimonies about Christians winning victories in a diversity of situations can be found online and in books. In order to gain these victories, believers have put on their spiritual clothing in one form or another. The "word of their testimony" (Revelation 12:11) confirms the faithfulness of God to his Word. My prayer for each reader of this book is that you will continue to have your testimony confirmed and established in Christ.

1 Corinthians 1:4-9 APNT
I give thanks to my God at all times on behalf of you for the grace of God that was given to you in Jesus Christ,
that in everything you may grow rich in him in every word and in all knowledge,
as the witness of Christ is established in you,
so that you do not lack in any one of his gifts, but you are waiting for the appearance of our Lord Jesus Christ,
who will establish you up to the end, so that you may be without blame in the day of our Lord Jesus Christ.
God is faithful, by whom you were called to the fellowship of his Son, Jesus Christ, our Lord.

"Established" means "to be strengthened or made firm." That is the purpose of this book – that we can learn more about standing and utilizing the armor of victory in every situation.

Before my conclusion regarding the armor, I want to address one question that I am often asked.

IS PRAYER ANOTHER PIECE OF THE ARMOR?

A number of teachers have suggested that there is another piece of the armor, which is prayer.[47] This is based on a valid point. The Roman soldier had another weapon called the **pilum**, a javelin commonly used by the Roman army in ancient times. It was about six feet long overall and was made of iron. It was used to throw at the enemy lines before actual engagement in combat. If prayer were named as another piece of the armor, there would have been a perfect comparison with the pilum.

This idea that prayer is another piece of the armor is also based on the verse that immediately follows the section on the armor of God in Ephesians 6.

Ephesians 6:18 APNT
And with all prayers and with all petitions, pray at all times spiritually, and in prayer, be watchful in every season, praying continually and interceding for all the holy [ones],

There is no question that this exhortation to pray is important in our Christian lives. In fact, all of the different kinds of prayer are mentioned in this one verse: devotional prayer, specific petition, praying in the Spirit, and intercession. But prayer is not compared to the javelin. Because it is not listed as a specific piece of the armor, we should not try to make it one.

It is also true that we need to pray in order to grow up into him in the whole spiritual walk. For this reason, I am convinced that this verse on prayer is a conclusion to the entire second half of the book of Ephesians. It is the crowning exhortation on what to do in our lives to "walk worthy of the calling" (Ephesians 4:1). Without praying fervently and "at all times" – and then LISTENING to God's response to our prayers – we will not be able to walk in balance, walk

---

[47] Priscilla Shirer, *The Armor of God*, p. 36.

in love or walk circumspectly. We must learn to be wise, and not foolish.

Finally, as stated in the chapter on *Our Spiritual Clothing*, the Ephesians section on the armor of God is set in the context of all we are in Christ (Ephesians 1-3) and how to live and walk (Ephesians 4-6) using what we have been given spiritually. Paul is the example of being diligent to pray for others in Ephesians, and exhorting the believers to pray in other passages in the epistles. His example makes it clear that the believer will need prayer to be able to live. Here are several passages to consider.

Ephesian 1:15-19 KJV
Wherefore I also, after I heard of your faith in the Lord Jesus, and love unto all the saints,
Cease not to give thanks for you, making mention of you in my prayers;
That the God of our Lord Jesus Christ, the Father of glory, may give unto you the spirit of wisdom and revelation in the knowledge of him:
The eyes of your understanding being enlightened; that ye may know what is the hope of his calling, and what the riches of the glory of his inheritance in the saints,
And what is the exceeding greatness of his power to usward who believe, according to the working of his mighty power.

Philippians 4:6 ESV
Do not be anxious about anything, but in everything by prayer and supplication with thanksgiving let your requests be made known to God.

1 Thessalonians 5:17 APNT
And pray unceasingly.

Colossians 4:2-3 KJV
Continue in prayer, and watch in the same with thanksgiving;

Withal praying also for us, that God would open unto us a door of
utterance, to speak the mystery of Christ, for which I am also in
bonds:

All the different kinds of prayer mentioned above (devotional prayer,
specific petition, praying in the Spirit, and intercession) are a vital
part of our relationship with God and the Lord Jesus Christ. No
Christian can consistently be victorious without asking for God's
guidance and help in prayer.

CONCLUSION

Ephesians 6:13 APNT
Because of this, put on the whole armor of God, so that you will be
able to engage the Evil [one] and, being prepared in everything, you
will stand firm.

The Greek word for "engage" or "withstand" (as in the King James
Version) is **antihistemi.** It is a compound word that means literally,
"stand against or stand opposite." We get our English word
"antihistamine" from this Greek word. Our bodies produce a
substance that "stands against" foreign invaders such as pollen; that
substance is called an antihistamine. We stand in this battle opposing
the army of the Evil One and resist his methods and tactics. The Evil
One can try to oppose us, but when we stand against his attack he has
to back down.

In this short record from Acts, Paul and Barnabas on their first
missionary journey stood against a man named Elymas who was a
sorcerer. Elymas was trying to prevent Sergius Paulus from hearing
the Word of God.

Acts 13:6-8 KJV
And when they had gone through the isle unto Paphos, they found a
certain sorcerer, a false prophet, a Jew, whose name was Barjesus:

Which was with the deputy of the country, Sergius Paulus, a prudent man; who called for Barnabas and Saul, and desired to hear the word of God.
But Elymas the sorcerer (for so is his name by interpretation) withstood them, seeking to turn away the deputy from the faith.

This obstruction by Elymas must have been going on for a period of time. Elymas is called a false prophet. Paul, filled with the Spirit, received the revelation that in addition to using deception, Elymas was also under the direction of a power, the spirit of perversion.

Acts 13:9-11 KJV
Then Saul, (who also is called Paul), filled with the Holy Ghost, set his eyes on him,
And said, O full of all subtilty [deceit] and all mischief, thou child of the devil, thou enemy of all righteousness, wilt thou not cease to pervert the right ways of the Lord?
And now, behold, the hand of the Lord is upon thee, and thou shalt be blind, not seeing the sun for a season. And immediately there fell on him a mist and a darkness; and he went about seeking some to lead him by the hand.
Then the deputy, when he saw what was done, believed, being astonished at the doctrine of the Lord.

God showed Paul how to deal with Elymas with astounding results and the deputy was astonished by the power of God that he saw in operation. Paul spoke what God had shown him – Elymas was under the influence of the Accuser. He was also filled with deceit (the Serpent) and perversion (Belial). God showed Paul what to do to resist. Then the Devil and his underlings had to flee.

James 4:7 KJV
Submit yourselves therefore to God. Resist the devil, and he will flee from you.

1 Peter 5:8-9 APNT
Be watchful and remember, because your enemy, Satan, roars as a lion and walks about and seeks whom he may swallow.

Therefore, stand against him, being steadfast in faith and know that these sufferings also happen to your brothers who are in the world.

RESIST, stand against the Evil One! Stand firm (steadfast) and do not be shaken by his roar! Remember the verses in Romans 8 that affirm the truth of our complete victory in very dire circumstances.

Romans 8:31-37 NET
What then shall we say about these things? If God is for us, who can be against us?
Indeed, he who did not spare his own Son, but gave him up for us all – how will he not also, along with him, freely give us all things?
Who will bring any charge against God's elect? It is God who justifies.
Who is the one who will condemn? Christ is the one who died (and more than that, he was raised), who is at the right hand of God, and who also is interceding for us.
Who will separate us from the love of Christ? Will trouble, or distress, or persecution, or famine, or nakedness, or danger, or sword?
As it is written, "For your sake we encounter death all day long; we were considered as sheep to be slaughtered."
No, in all these things we have complete victory through him who loved us!

We are not sheep led to slaughter! On the contrary, nothing can separate us from God who justifies, nor from Christ who died for us. Because we have all the enablements given to us in Christ, "having done all," stand firm (Ephesians 6:13).

Priscilla Shirer, the author of a group Bible study called *The Armor of God*, points out that we need to stop living passive lives offering no resistance to the Enemy.

> Our enemy celebrates lethargic Christian living. When we're giving up on relationships, disregarding the purity of our reputations, yielding to our appetites without putting up much, if any resistance, he can basically go unchecked. Wreak havoc in the lives of God's people. Ultimately, he can

hamstring the church from achieving the purposes of God. Our indolence and inertia work to his great advantage, practically rolling out the red carpet for his entrance into the unlocked doors of our indifference and despondency. He's hardly going to pass up an opening like that.[48]

Living this life without active resistance to the Enemy is comparable to walking naked into a raging snowstorm. You would never expect to survive the snowstorm. The Amplified Version of Ephesians 4 summarizes how to put on our spiritual clothing.

Ephesians 4:20-24 AMPC
But you did not learn Christ in this way!
If in fact you have [really] heard Him and have been taught by Him, just as truth is in Jesus [revealed in His life and personified in Him], that, regarding your previous way of life, you put off your old self [completely discard your former nature], which is being corrupted through deceitful desires,
and be continually renewed in the spirit of your mind [having a fresh, untarnished mental and spiritual attitude],
and put on the new self [the regenerated and renewed nature], created in God's image, [godlike] in the righteousness and holiness of the truth [living in a way that expresses to God your gratitude for your salvation].

Strip off the old man, putting off the old ways of thinking. Then, put on the new man – the Lord Jesus Christ. Remember that our armor is summarized in these three names. Jesus is LORD. That means he is the boss, master, the one who has first place. Jesus is the Deliverer, Savior, the one who shed his blood to pay for all our sins and shortcomings. Yeshua, Jesus' name in Aramaic, is similar to Joshua, the great general who led the armies of God into the Promised Land. Christ is the risen, glorified, and anointed one who is seated at the right hand of the throne of God. He sent his Spirit of holiness to indwell every believer so that we would have everything that we need to be victorious.

---

[48] Priscilla Shirer, *The Armor of God,* p. 24.

Colossians 2:10 KJV
And ye are complete in him, which is the head of all principality and power:

In Aramaic, "ye are complete" is in an unusual extensive and passive tense called Eshtaphal. The simple verb means "to fill;" when it is used in this tense it means "absolutely completed" or "completely supplied." We are supplied with everything we need in Christ!

Whatever your battle, the Lord God who rescued you from the powers of darkness is the same Lord who comes to deliver you from the hand of the Enemy. Consider David's revelation about God and pray this verse for yourself.

Psalm 18:17-19 NASB
He delivered me from my strong enemy, And from those who hated me, for they were too mighty for me.
They confronted me in the day of my calamity, But the LORD was my stay.
He brought me forth also into a broad place; He rescued me, because He delighted in me.

Here is another promise:

Isaiah 49:24 ESV
Can the prey be taken from the mighty, or the captives of a tyrant be rescued?
For thus says the LORD: "Even the captives of the mighty shall be taken, and the prey of the tyrant be rescued, for I will contend with those who contend with you, and I will save your children."

We have been delivered from the authority of darkness and transferred into the kingdom of God's beloved Son. Therefore, we can have strength, knowing we are rescued and redeemed.

Colossians 1:11-14 APNT
*[And that you] may be strengthened with all strength, according to
the greatness of his glory. With all patience and long-suffering and
with joy,*
*you should give thanks to God the Father, who has made us worthy
for a portion of the inheritance of the holy [ones] in light.*
*and has delivered us from the authority of darkness and has
transferred us to the kingdom of his beloved Son,*
in whom we have redemption and forgiveness of sins.

We need to stand fast in the freedom for which Christ freed us, stand
firm in our place in the body of Christ, and stand in victory clothed
in the armor of God.

Galatians 5:1 APNT
*Stand fast, therefore, in the freedom [for] which Christ freed us and
do not be subjected again with the yoke of bondage.*

Today we do not fight for victory; we fight from victory. We do not
fight in order to win; in Christ we have already won. Those who stand
in victory rest in the victory already given to them in Christ. We stand
on the ground already won by our Captain of Salvation. Put on the
whole armor of God – our spiritual clothing – and our weapons in the
Lord Jesus Christ, and stand in victory. Resist all the plans and
purposes of the Evil One with determination and courage. We are
strengthened in our Lord and the power of his might. We stand with
the whole ARMOR OF VICTORY!

Appendix
Other Names of the Evil One

Angel of Light	2 Corinthians 11:14
Despiser	Revelation 12:10
Devourer	Malachi 3:11
Enemy	Matthew 13:39, Luke 10:19
Father of lies	John 8:44
God of this world	2 Corinthians 4:4
Murderer	John 8:44
Prince	Daniel 10:20
Prince of the power of the air	Ephesians 2:2
Prince of this world	John 12:31, 14:30, 16:11
Roaring Lion	1 Peter 5:8
Tempter	Matthew 4:3, 1 Thessalonians 3:5
Thief	John 10:10

Bibliography

Anderson, Neil T. *Victory over the Darkness*. Ventura, California: Regal Books, 1990.

Barker, Kenneth, et al. *The NIV Study Bible*. Grand Rapids, Michigan: Zondervan Publishing House, 1995.

Benner, Jeff A. *The Ancient Hebrew Lexicon of the Bible*. College Station, Texas: Virtualbookworm.com Publishing, 2005.

Bevere, John. *The Bait of Satan*. Lake Mary, Florida: Creation House, 2014.

Bevere, John. *The Devil's Door*. Lake Mary, Florida: Creation House, 1982.

Bevere, John. *Breaking Intimidation*. Orlando, Florida: Creation House, 1995.

Brooks, Thomas. *Precious Remedies Against Satan's Devices*. Edinburgh: The Banner of Truth Trust, first published in 1652, 1997.

Brown, Francis, S.R. Driver, Charles A. Briggs, eds. *The New Brown-Driver-Briggs-Gesenius Hebrew and English Lexicon*. Christian Copyrights, Inc., 1983.

Brown, Raymond E., Joseph A. Fitzmyer, Roland E. Murphy. *The Jerome Biblical Commentary*. Englewood Cliffs, New Jersey: Prentice-Hall, Inc., 1968.

Brown, Rebecca. *Unbroken Curses*. Springdale, Pennsylvania: Whitaker House, 1995.

Bullinger, E. W. *A Critical Lexicon and Concordance to the English and Greek New Testament*. Grand Rapids, Michigan: Zondervan Publishing House, 1975.

Bullinger, E.W., *Figures of Speech Used in the Bible*. Grand Rapids, Michigan: Baker Book House, 1968.

BIBLIOGRAPHY

Chafer, Lewis Sperry. *Satan His Motive and Methods.* Grand Rapids, Michigan: Zondervan Publishing House, 1971.

Clarke, Adam. *The New Testament of our Lord and Saviour Jesus Christ, Commentary on the Bible.* New York: Abingdon Press. Volumes 1-6.

Douglas, J. D, ed. *New Bible Dictionary.* Wheaton, Illinois: Tyndale House Publishers, 1987.

Ellicott, Charles, ed. *The Layman's Handy Commentary on the Bible,* Epistles to the Galatians, Ephesians and Philippians. Grand Rapids, Michigan: Zondervan Publishing House, 1957.

Foss, Steve. *Satan's Dirty Little Secret.* Lake Mary, Florida: Charisma House, 2012.

Frangipane, Francis. *Exposing the Accuser of the Brethren.* Cedar Rapids, Iowa: Arrow Publications, 1991.

Frangipane, Francis. *This Day We Fight!* Grand Rapids, Michigan: Chosen Books, 2007.

Gaebelein, Frank, ed. *The Expositor's Bible Commentary, Volume II.* Grand Rapids, Michigan: Zondervan Publishing House, 1978.

Gurnall, William. *The Christian in Complete Armor,* 3 volumes. Edinburgh: The Banner of Truth Trust, first published in 1655, 1996.

Hammond, Frank. *Overcoming Rejection.* Kirkwood, Michigan: Impact Christian Books, 1987.

Hammond, Frank. *Pigs in the Parlor.* Kirkwood, Michigan: Impact Christian Books, 1973.

Harris, R. Laird, Gleason L. Archer, Jr., Bruce K. Waltke, eds. *Theological Wordbook of the Old Testament,* 2 volumes. Chicago, Illinois: Moody Press, 1980.

Jacobs, Cindy. *Possessing the Gates of the Enemy.* Grand Rapids, Michigan: Chosen Books, 1991.

BIBLIOGRAPHY

Jakes, T.D. *Woman, Thou Art Loosed!* Shippensburg, Pennsylvania: Destiny Image Publishers, 1993.

Jennings, William. *Lexicon to the Syriac New Testament.* London: Oxford University Press, 1926.

Jeremiah, David. *Slaying the Giants in Your Life.* Nashville, Tennessee: W. Publishing Group, 2001.

Kleu, Michael and Madelene Eayrs. *Satan's Generals.* El Qana Ministries, 2011.

Lamsa, George M. *Gospel Light, A Revised Annotated Edition.* Aramaic Bible Society, 1999.

Larkin, Clarence. *The Spirit World.* Glenside, Pennsylvania: Rev. Clarence Larkin Estate, 1921.

Lightfoot, John. *A Commentary on the New Testament from the Talmud and Hebraica.* 4 volumes. Peabody, Massachusetts: Hendrickson Publishers, 1989.

Lloyd-Jones, D. Martyn. *The Christian Soldier.* Grand Rapids, Michigan: Baker Book House, 1989.

MacArthur, John Jr. *The Believer's Armor.* Chicago, Illinois: Moody Press, 1986.

Mathias, Art. *Biblical Foundations of Freedom.* Anchorage, Alaska: Wellspring Publishing, 2002.

Murdock, James, trans. *The New Testament.* New York: Stanford and Swords, 1852.

Nave, Orville J. *The New Nave's Topical Bible.* Grand Rapids, Michigan: Zondervan Publishing House, 1969.

Nee, Watchman. *Sit, Walk, Stand.* Carol Stream, Illinois: Tyndale House Publishers, 1977.

BIBLIOGRAPHY

Null, William G. *Rejection – Its Fruits and Its Roots.* Lake Hamilton Bible Camp, Hot Springs, Arkansas, 2005.

Page, Sydney. *Powers of Evil.* Grand Rapids, Michigan: Baker Book House, 1995.

Renner, Rick. *Dressed to Kill.* Tulsa, Oklahoma: Harrison House, 1991.

Prince, Derek. *They Shall Expel Demons.* Grand Rapids, Michigan: Chosen Books, 1998.

Renner, Rick. *Spiritual Weapons to Defeat the Enemy.* Tulsa, Oklahoma: Piliar Books & Publishing, 1993.

Rice, Edwin W. *People's Dictionary of the Bible.* Philadelphia, Pennsylvania: American Sunday School Union, 1904.

Richards, Larry. *The Full Armor of God.* Minneapolis, Minnesota: Chosen Books, 2013.

Ryken, Leland, ed. *Dictionary of Biblical Imagery.* Downers Grove, Illinois: InterVarsity Press, 1998.

Savard, Liberty. *Shattering Your Strongholds.* North Brunswick, New Jersey: Bridge-Logos Publishers, 1992.

Shirer, Priscilla. *The Armor of God.* Nashville, Tennessee: LifeWay Press, 2016.

Silvoso, Ed. *That None Should Perish.* Ventura, California: Regal Books, 1994.

Smith, J. Payne. *A Compendious Syriac Dictionary.* London: Oxford at the Clarendon Press, 1967.

Stone, Perry. *There's a Crack in Your Armor.* Lake Mary, Florida: Charisma House, 2014.

Suddreth, Betty Green. *Who Are the Strong Men Over Our Nation.* Hudson, North Carolina.

BIBLIOGRAPHY

Thayer, Joseph Henry. *The New Thayer's Greek-English Lexicon of the New Testament*. Christian Copyrights, Inc., 1981.

Van der Toorn, Karel, ed. *Dictionary of Deities and Demons in the Bible*. Grand Rapids, Michigan: William B. Eerdmans Publishing Co., 1999.

Unger, Merrill F. *Biblical Demonology*. Wheaton, Illinois: Scripture Press, 1970.

Unger, Merrill F. *Unger's Bible Dictionary*. Chicago, Illinois: Moody Press, 1974.

Vincent, Marvin R. *Word Studies in the New Testament*, 4 volumes. Grand Rapids, Michigan: William B. Eerdmans Publishing Co., 1946.

Wagner, Peter and Douglas Pennoyer, eds. *Wrestling with Dark Angels*. Ventura, California: Regal Books, 1990.

Webster, Noah, *Noah Webster's first Edition of An American Dictionary of the English Language*. San Francisco: Foundation for American Christian Education, 1967.

Welch, Charles, *The Testimony of the Lord's Prisoner*. London: The Berean Publishing Trust, 1931.

Wiersbe, Warren. *The Strategy of Satan*. Wheaton, Illinois: Tyndale House Publishers, 1979.

Wink, Walter, *Naming the Powers*. Philadelphia, Pennsylvania: Fortress Press, 1984.

Wright, Henry W. *A More Excellent Way to Be in Health*. New Kensington, Pennsylvania: Whitaker House, 2009.

ABOUT THE AUTHOR

Janet Magiera is an ordained minister and the founder of Light of the Word Ministry, a ministry dedicated to teaching and making known the understanding of the Aramaic language, figures of speech and customs of the Bible. In 1979, under the tutelage of a student of Dr. George M. Lamsa, Jan began pursuing a course of study of the Aramaic Peshitta New Testament. For over 50 years, she has taught in Bible fellowships and churches in the United States and other countries, using insight from her understanding of the Biblical languages. Many articles and teachings of interest are available on the Light of the Word Ministry website, www.lightofword.org.

In 1990, Jan began compiling a database of the Aramaic Peshitta New Testament. As computer technology increased over the years, she expanded and developed the database to generate a series of research tools to study the New Testament. The entire database is now available online at www.aramaicdb.org. The *Aramaic Peshitta New Testament Translation* was the first book published in 2006 of a complete *Aramaic Peshitta New Testament Library*. The library includes a 3-volume interlinear, lexicon, concordance, and parallel translations. There is an app of the Aramaic translation on both ITunes and GooglePlay, as well as various electronic versions of her books and the translations.

Jan has also authored several topical books on Biblical subjects including *Enriched in Everything* on giving; and *Members in Particular* on the body of Christ. Other titles are *The Coming of the Son of Man; The Fence of Salvation; Ephesians: Our Spiritual Treasure; and Our Walk in Christ.*

She currently lives in Colorado Springs, Colorado.

www.ingramcontent.com/pod-product-compliance
Lightning Source LLC
Chambersburg PA
CBHW071445090426
42737CB00011B/1780